THE AWAKENED LIFE

The Law of Attraction

DIANE AHLQUIST

ALPHA

A member of Penguin Random House LLC

Publisher: Mike Sanders
Senior Acquisitions Editor: Janette Lynn
Book Producer: Lee Ann Chearneyi/Amaranth@LuminAreStudio.com
Art Director: William Thomas
Copy Editor: Monica Stone
Cover Designer: Jessica Lee
Book Designer/Layout: Ayanna Lacey
Indexer: Brad Herriman
Proofreader: Lisa Starnes

This book is dedicated to Daniel Frenden, who has dedicated himself unselfishly to others so that they have better lives. Your mother raised you well. And although your father, John, has made the transition from Vietnam-related issues, he is very proud of you. We all love you!

International Standard Book Number: 978-1-46549-012-4
Library of Congress Catalog Card Number: 2019945958

Interpretation of the printing code: The rightmost number of the first series of numbers is the year of the book's printing; the rightmost number of the second series of numbers is the number of the book's printing. For example, a printing code of 19-1 shows that the first printing occurred in 2019.

Printed in the United States of America

Note: This publication contains the opinions and ideas of its authors. It is intended to provide helpful and informative material on the subject matter covered. It is sold with the understanding that the authors and publisher are not engaged in rendering professional services in the book. If the reader requires personal assistance or advice, a competent professional should be consulted. The authors and publisher specifically disclaim any responsibility for any liability, loss, or risk, personal or otherwise, which is incurred as a consequence, directly or indirectly, of the use and application of any of the contents of this book.

Most Alpha books are available at special quantity discounts for bulk purchases for sales promotions, premiums, fund-raising, or educational use. Special books, or book excerpts, can also be created to fit specific needs. For details, write: Special Markets, Alpha Books, 1450 Broadway, Suite 801, New York, NY 10018.

Trademarks: All terms mentioned in this book that are known to be or are suspected of being trademarks or service marks have been appropriately capitalized. Alpha Books and Penguin Random House LLC cannot attest to the accuracy of this information. Use of a term in this book should not be regarded as affecting the validity of any trademark or service mark.

Reprinted and updated from *The Complete Idiot's Guide to the Law of Attraction*

A WORLD OF IDEAS:
SEE ALL THERE IS TO KNOW

www.dk.com
First American Edition, 2019

Contents

Part 5: Review Your Work   189

Appendixes

Introduction

If you can think it, feel it, and believe it, you're in. In what? In with the universe and the understanding that you can attract whatever you want in life.

There is a universal law—the law of attraction—that says we draw near to us the things we think about most. If you focus on the things you want, you will get them. But if you spend most of your time thinking about what you *don't* want, you get those things, too. So positive thoughts and positive intention are the keys to a happy, healthy life.

Now, I know you're saying, "Diane, if it were that easy, everybody would already have what they want, and no one would be unhappy!" Well, it is that easy; people just tend to lose sight of the feeling and believing aspects of the law of attraction. Attracting what you want is far less complicated than you think, and you're doing it all the time, whether you realize it or not. Are you wondering why you're faced with difficult situations and difficult people all the time? It could be that these are the things drawing your (negative) energy and attention; by default (because you aren't consciously asking for it), the universe sends more of the same back to you. If you've spent years wondering what you have been doing wrong, this book may be the key to your understanding.

Mastering the law of attraction will lead you to a happy, healthy, prosperous, spiritual life, if this is your inclination. The important thing is for you to *know* what you want in advance. And, hey, even if you do change your mind along the way, we can fix that, too. Is it a miracle cure to create a wonderful life? Nope, no miracle, just a universal law that you may not have been aware of.

Humans have practiced these methods knowingly or unknowingly since the beginning of time. Now it's your turn. What's it going to be: a positive outcome or a negative one? It's all up to you!

How This Book Is Organized

I've divided this book into five easy-to-digest portions that will lead you through the concepts of the law of attraction and how to put the law to good use in your daily life. I suggest taking the time to focus on one chapter at a time before moving on. This information is like building blocks; you use each piece to make the foundation and the structure stronger.

Part 1, The Universal Law of Attraction Defined and Demystified, gets into the specifics of the law of attraction: what is it, where did it come from, and why is it suddenly all the rage these days? You'll also learn about other universal laws and why they always hold true. Finally, you'll read why the law of attraction tends to work very well for some folks and not at all for others. The secret is that it works for everyone; but you get what you focus on most, and if that happens to be something negative … guess what's going to come your way?

Part 2, Can You Feel It? discusses important skills for using the law of attraction. The issue of "want" vs. "don't want" is of the utmost importance here, but using positive language, believing, and focusing on your request are important, too. I'll also talk about compassion and its role in the law of attraction.

Part 3, What Goes Around Comes Around, talks about the specifics of appealing to the universe, visualizing a positive outcome, and allowing what you've asked for into your life. Sneaky self-sabotage methods are covered in this section, as are methods for overcoming them. I've also included a section on educating your children to make the most positive choices in life and to use the most positive language possible, so that they won't have to undo the negative energy we adults tend to focus on!

Part 4, People, Places, and Intents, gets into the nitty-gritty that people are so curious about: can you make someone love you? What kind of vibe should you send to a backstabbing friend? I'll also discuss methods for acing job interviews, planning for a first date, and bringing a new home into your life. Discover how social media arouses both positive and negative emotions and how to handle it! I'll also give you ideas for attracting wonderful things to our great big home, Earth. What you see in your mind, you'll bring to your reality, so prepare to welcome the best of the best!

Part 5, Review Your Work covers common errors in using the law of attraction and offers trouble-shooting advice for "repairing" your request. You'll also learn why more isn't necessarily merrier as far as the law of attraction is concerned, along with methods for helping other people with your intent and positive energy.

Acknowledgments

To all of you who are reading this, be it a physical book, an e-book, or by audio, you attracted it into your life, so enjoy what you initiated.

As always, thank you to my entire family: My sister, lovely Marie; and Rosemarie, my mother, who is always calm and understanding. To Johnny, my favorite oldest nephew; enchanting Lori; Dan; and special blessings to those handsome guys Joshua and Ethen Frenden. Bob Irwin, so many blessings for all of your help through the years! We all love you. Yes, we do!

Bron, Christine, Myka, Marco, and Shane, your constant support is precious. Valentina, when you start to read and have a few years behind you, I am sure you will love this book!

Let's not forget to thank the hubby, Adrian Volney, for all his love and support. I attracted a keeper! Not a cook, but a handsome and wonderful person—not to mention a boater!

To Chris Shake, for finding us, and vice versa. Someone who "gets it," he is intelligence at its finest.

To Christine Soderbeck, for your encouragement and positive attitude. Good job on Bay Watch! And she can cook!

To David Stahl, "It's a good day!"

To Janet Osterholt, the only woman who can tend to her garden and still look vgood. It's just not fair! PS: Don't forget to drizzle crème de menthe on top of the cake. And, of course, to Steve, her handsome husband, who makes a wicked Brandy Alexander!

To Shelly Hagen, I did a really good job bringing you into my reality. Thank you for your involvement!

To everyone at Penguin Random House and Alpha who contributed to this book, especially Jan Lynn.

Trademarks

All terms mentioned in this book that are known to be or are suspected of being trademarks or service marks have been appropriately capitalized. Alpha Books and Penguin Random House LLC cannot attest to the accuracy of this information. Use of a term in this book should not be regarded as affecting the validity of any trademark or service mark.

PART I

The Universal Law of Attraction Defined and Demystified

The law of attraction is nothing new; in fact, it's been around and in use since the dawn of humanity. So what kinds of new things can you learn about an ancient method of self-help? Plenty. In these chapters, I introduce you to the basic elements of this universal law and put you on the right track to begin asking the universe or source energy for all that you desire!

CHAPTER 1

There Ought to Be a Law ...

There's been a lot of talk in the last few years about the law of attraction. Some people say that this idea has helped them shape their happy and successful lives, while other people are doubtful that the power of positive thought can have much of an effect on big issues, like landing the right job or finding Mr. or Ms. Right. I say that your mind is the most powerful tool you have, as far as planning your future goes.

The law of attraction isn't something that a trendy L.A. guru dreamed up a few years back—it's something that's been used for centuries! To understand why your friends and family are diving headfirst into this teaching, you'll need to understand its origin. This chapter will give you an overview of where the law of attraction began, where it's going, and what it can do for you.

Ancient Universal Secret, Huh?

In order to use the universal law of attraction to your benefit, you must have a solid understanding of this principle. I know, I know, you want to get to the meat (the "how to") of the book, but as with anything that is worthwhile, you must first learn the basics of how it works. This information will help everything else make sense and make your journey more logical.

Sending Out the Vibe

The *law of attraction* describes the flow of energy between each person and the universe. Positive thoughts and attitudes draw positive energy from the universe, while negative beliefs vibrate to attract negative results.

We are all made up of energy and, as you know, energy can never be destroyed, only changed. Our thoughts are also energy. Some experts in the law of attraction liken the energy of your thoughts to the way electrons behave around the nucleus of an atom. (I'm not a scientist, by the way, so this discussion will be pretty light and easy.)

All matter is made of atoms, so all matter also contains electrons. Every atom has a certain number of electrons which rotate around the nucleus of the atom. Long story short: the electrons vibrate at a higher level if more energy (say, heat) is added to the atom. With enough energy, the atoms will line up and the electrons will produce a "pulling" effect—moving the atoms.

The theory goes that because we are all made of atoms, high energy (positive energy, that is) can produce a similar pulling effect in which our thoughts transmit energy outside of ourselves. And where does the energy go? Out to the universe, which is chock-full of energy, and it sends back the same sort of energy we sent out in the first place. This is why attitudes and events tend to be reinforced—they come right back to us. If you believe something bad is going to happen at work tomorrow, for example, it probably will; on the other hand, if you expect to have a great day in the office, you probably won't be disappointed!

So, is the law of attraction a scientific or spiritual practice? Some say it's both. Subscribing to the theory that we're all energy isn't enough; you also need to have faith that your intent can bring good things into your life.

Where Did This Idea Come From?

The law of attraction has been around since the beginning of time. This is not a new concept or a trendy thought. It is old news. In fact, it is ancient news.

The law of attraction is a *universal law*, meaning a principle that applies to the entire universe and is considered the bedrock of being and nature. I'll talk about the universal laws in detail in Chapter 2.

You may be wondering who discovered the law of attraction. Was it one person or a group? Even though it has always existed, someone had to discover it (or at least name it) so it could be passed on through the generations, right? Who exactly was this person?

Good question. The answer is that no one person discovered it; people just started using it, consciously or unconsciously, and it worked for them, so they passed on their methods to their children and so on through the centuries. Artists, musicians, scholars, leaders, and ordinary folk were smart enough to recognize and use the flow of the universe to their advantage.

Look at the teachings, thoughts, or poetry of those who we have deemed to be great figures, both present and past. Maybe we don't all agree on who the most brilliant men and women were—for example, there are those who think Albert Einstein was a genius and others who think he is highly overrated. But no matter what you think of him, he understood the law of attraction. Investigate Socrates and Ben Franklin. Famed self-improvement guru Dale Carnegie even says, "The ideas I stand for are not mine. I borrowed them from Socrates. I swiped them from Chesterfield. I stole them from Jesus .... If you don't like their rules, whose would you use?"

Look to composers, such as Mozart, and artists you love and respect. They attracted beautiful and healing music and art into their lives—and we share in the benefits, just as the universe has always intended.

Modern Lives Based on Long-Standing Knowledge

We can see the law of attraction at work in our everyday lives. Every time we turn on the television, talk to a friend, or just reflect on our personal lives, we're dealing with the law of attraction. It's everywhere and always in action, whether positive or negative.

We have seen motivational speakers talk about the power of being positive and associating with positive, like-minded people to help us achieve success. The speakers are actually talking about the law of attraction, the whole "birds of a feather flock together" concept.

Take a look at inspirational speakers such as Zig Ziglar or Eric Thomas, who leave audiences filled with energy and hope at the end of a presentation. Their positive vibe is downright infectious. Unfortunately, that hope and happiness often wear off after a few days because those who attended don't take the time to tap into their positive energy sources. They fall back into their negative mindsets and nothing really changes in their lives.

So, the trick is to keep the positive energy going and to send calm vibrations out to the universe, so that in return, you'll receive the things you really want. This is all very possible simply by using the law of attraction.

The Resurgence of Attraction Principles

I am neither the first writer nor will I be the last to write about the law of attraction. But because so many people are only now discovering this concept and seeing the positive changes it can make in their lives, they are genuinely revved up about it. Their focus and desire for information brings forth more information, and more sharing of that information draws more people in and gets *them* excited! The positive-thinking attitudes keep snowballing.

People have become excited about this old concept due to the success of books such as *The Secret* by Rhonda Byrne and the *The Law of Attraction: The Basics of the Teachings of Abraham* by Esther and Jerry Hicks. (For more information on these books and other resources, make sure to read through Appendix B.)

I think the best part of this whole resurgence is how it spreads by word of mouth from people who have used it and found happiness by doing so—and *anyone* can find success using this principle, whether that person is a stock clerk or an executive. This means very diverse populations are telling friends and acquaintances how their lives are changing, and the friends and acquaintances are giving these ideas some credence ... and the movement continues to spread and experience an incredible rebirth.

Your Personal Power Source

Your mind is stronger than you think. Moreover, it has a direct connection to the universe, which responds to your strongest, clearest thoughts (whether they're positive or negative). Until you acknowledge this, it may be difficult for you to invest your time and energy into using the law of attraction to your benefit.

The law of attraction teaches us that there is enough happiness and success for everyone on the planet, so there is no need and no room for jealousy or feeling slighted. If there's one catch to this law, it's this: the way you think—and the type of energy you transmit—shapes your entire life, from the smallest incidents right on up to the events that change the way you view the world. Change the way you think and you may find that you have a whole new existence on your hands!

Fair warning: to attract good things into your life, you have to be willing to evaluate the sources of negativity in your life. Why hang out with friends who are always negative and pessimistic? Their energy literally rubs off on you, changing the way you feel about life and affecting the energy you send out to the universe. If you can't cut ties with these people altogether, then you'll need to work hard on not absorbing their cynicism.

Your Life, Your Creation

Are you generally a happy person or a cantankerous person?

Do you love your job or hate it?

Are you comfortable with your financial situation?

How's your health these days?

What kinds of friends and relationships do you have?

If you aren't pleased with your answers to these questions, there is an explanation—and it's not your boss, or the fact you had to file for bankruptcy, or because you got food poisoning after eating oysters with those friends who are always talking you into doing something you don't want to do.

The reason you aren't happy is … you. You made your life. You hear this all over the media—in books, classes, seminars, and so forth. We have each created ourselves, our entire lives, and every emotion that goes along with it—the whole enchilada.

Most people agree with this to a certain extent but try to find some "outs," like "I can see that maybe I created a situation at my job I don't like because I didn't quit when I should have. But it wasn't my fault I fell off my bike into that ditch of cow manure yesterday." Well, actually, you created the fall into the cow manure. And, if you are thinking *this* idea is cow manure, please read on.

You Are What You Think

Observe the way other people talk about their lives, not mentioning anything to them about the law of attraction. Do you notice that their predictions tend to come true? Your positive-minded friends tend to draw joy to themselves, while your friends with negative attitudes find themselves in sorry situations, time and time again.

What about the way *you* think about situations?

Let's say you're pedaling on a road bordering a cow-manure ditch, which is a great metaphor for many situations in life. There's going to be stuff on the periphery that you definitely don't want to be in the middle of … so how do you stay out?

Well, if you keep thinking "I'd better not fall into that stinky ditch," you are sending out a certain kind of vibration. As you continue your ride and you keep looking at the ditch and thinking about what would happen if you fell in, you are drawing that situation into your life. So—poof! Down you go! The universe hears "fall into … stinky ditch" backed by a negative emotion, and it delivers on that strong negativity.

Let's take a look at how things could have gone differently. Let's even say in this example that your bike is in terrible repair with a tire that keeps losing air, a chain that keeps falling off, and brakes that are iffy. Logically, you have a pretty good chance of swerving into that ditch while riding such a machine, right? But if you sincerely think to yourself, "No matter what happens and how bad a condition this bike is in, I just never fall." Well, the universe hears "I never fall." And guess what? You pedal right past the stink and come out smelling like roses. This is also a situation that you have created with your own thoughts!

Of course, every thought does not manifest instantly. Most take time and effort to develop into reality. We'll discuss this later in the book.

Change the Channel!

This is a good time to talk about programming. I'm not talking about that TV show you love to watch; I'm talking about the conclusions your mind automatically jumps to in a given situation. You've been programmed to respond in certain ways. That response sends a negative or positive vibe, and *voilà*! You keep repeating the same situations over and over again.

Programming refers to the thoughts we're trained to believe about ourselves and the world around us, even though they may not be true. It begins when you're a child. If someone ever said to you, "You're not smart enough to win that award," or, "You're so ugly, no one will ever date you," and you believed it, it's part of your programming. Programming can also work in the opposite way. Some little girls really believe they're princesses, for example, because their parents have told them that they are!

So, how does programming work with the law of attraction? It affects every part of it! Here's an example:

- ♦ When you believe you aren't worthy of a promotion because you're not very smart (something you "learned" in childhood), you won't ask for it.
- ♦ If by some miracle, you do ask the universe for a promotion, you don't believe you will get it.
- ♦ If, by another miracle, you get the promotion and don't believe you deserve it, you will likely not succeed in the new position and find yourself right back where you started.

The universe isn't into delivering things that people are wishy-washy on. You have to know with all of your heart that you are deserving and that anything can happen—regardless of what you were taught as a child.

So, before you go any further with this process, sit down and think about the negative things you say to and about yourself every day. Write them down. Acknowledge that they are not the truth, just something that someone once told you. (People tell untruths all the time. I could tell you that I'm Marie Antoinette—would you believe me?) And then work to deprogram yourself. You can do this by saying something as simple as, "I am smart. I do deserve a promotion." But you have to be consistent (don't lapse back into your old beliefs), and you have to *mean* it. Even if you don't believe it 100 percent at first, keep saying it with confidence. Before long, you'll find that you've replaced old, negative beliefs with positive, new convictions. What you get from the law of attraction depends on your outlook, so keep working at having the most positive attitude that you can muster!

You Manifest Your Destiny

Even if you don't believe any of this, just pretend you do for a moment. Go back to situations where you assumed a negative outcome before it even happened, such as "I just know I'm going to be late for my meeting." It seems it's so much easier to believe in the negative than the positive! When you say something negative to yourself—like you're going to be late—you invest a strong negative energy in that thought. You worry; you're anxious; you start to falter in other areas. In this case, perhaps you aren't as sharp doing your morning tasks as you would be if you were in a positive mindset. This makes you run late. By the time you're finished, it's raining, you can't catch a cab, and guess what? You're late for your meeting.

This is obviously a minor example, but the law of attraction works in every area of your life, whether you acknowledge it or not. Here are some particularly damaging statements:

"I always attract losers."

"People think I'm boring."

"I'll never get ahead in my finances."

"I'll be stuck in this job I hate forever."

When you say things like this to yourself over and over again, the universe picks up your attitude (your energy) and gives you exactly what you expect. So, stop doing this to yourself! Give the universe a chance to send you what you want! Begin by preparing to change your mind-set, and the future will take care of itself.

CHAPTER 2

Universal Laws: Don't Violate Them!

The minute we see or hear the word *law*, it usually gives us the feeling that we'd better be on our best behavior or we could be in trouble. And we think of those who uphold the law (police, judges, and other authority figures) as rather intimidating folks. But within the confines of this book, when I talk about *law*, I'm not talking about getting a ticket or paying your debt to society. I am talking about universal law.

When I talk about universal law, you have to think outside the Earth box, so to speak. I'm talking about things that apply to all beings everywhere (if you believe in those sorts of things) and don't change with time. For example, today it may be law that you must park your car in a certain area and pay a certain amount of taxes on your property. These things are human laws; even though we should obey them, they don't reflect the essence (or energy) of who we are. Parking your car on the wrong side of the street usually doesn't affect the energy you send out to the universe. (Unless you do it on purpose for some spiteful reason … but that's another story altogether!) However, going against the Laws of the Universe can get you into some serious hot water!

The Law of Love

Some think that energy makes the world go 'round, and others think we have love to thank for that. But because love *is* energy, I think it's a combination of the two. Now some people might disagree and say, "I've never been in love, and I don't really love anybody. What difference does that make if I'm focused on the things I want to attract into my life?"

Well, it makes a big difference because we aren't talking about romantic love. We're talking more about showing concern and respect for your fellow human beings.

Here are some examples of religious and spiritual teachings that have this one theme in common:

◆ **Buddhism.** "Hurt not others with that which pains yourself." (Udanavarga 5.18)

◆ **Christianity.** "The entire law is summed up in a single command: love your neighbor as yourself." (Bible, Galatians 5:14)

◆ **Confucianism.** "Do not unto others what you would not they should do unto you." (Analects 15.23)

◆ **Hinduism.** "This is the sum of duty: do nothing to others which if done to you, would cause you pain." (Mahabharata 5.1517)

◆ **Islam.** "No one of you is a believer until he loves for his brother what he loves for himself." (Traditions)

◆ **Judaism.** "What is hurtful to yourself do not to your fellow man. That is the whole of the Torah and the remainder is but commentary. Go learn it." (Talmud)

◆ **Native American.** "Do not wrong or hate your neighbor. For it is not he who you wrong, but yourself." (Pima proverb)

◆ **Shintoism.** "Be charitable to all beings; love is the representative of God." (Ko-ji-ki Hachiman Kasuga)

◆ **Taoism.** "Regard your neighbor's loss as your own loss." (T'ai shang kan ying p'ien)

◆ **Wicca.** "An' it harm none, do what thou wilt." (Wiccan Rede)

Now some of these quotes are taken from religious texts, but others are from spiritual teachings that subscribe to the power of the universe. So, you don't have to be a regular church-goer to get this concept. What the law of love basically says is "Be good to others."

Even if you are an avowed atheist, there's some common sense and logic to loving your fellow human. It's more about a common energy that we put forth. The more people treat each other well, the more positive energy there is to share.

Acceptance

When demonstrating the law of love, we must also understand that even though we are all connected, we are not all alike. It's not always easy to accept someone who's very different from us—in appearance, in attitude, in beliefs, or whatever. This is when it's a real challenge for us to plug into our love circuit (as we'll call it for the moment) and shoot out some love energy!

My friend Annie had a tough time dealing with personalities within her own family. Her sister, Debbie, had always been rigid in her thoughts and actions. If Debbie believed something had to be done a certain way, then that was that. When the time came to clean out their aging parents' home, Debbie, as the eldest sibling, took the lead, texting and emailing orders to Annie and her brothers without regard to their work and family schedules. Annie recalls, "It wasn't that we didn't want to help—we all really wanted to be a part of helping our parents with this! But we needed to be able to say, 'I'm available this particular day, but definitely not this other day because I have to work, or because my kid has a play, or whatever the previous commitment was.'"

Debbie was having no part of this. She had made a schedule, and she was furious with her younger siblings for not accommodating her plan. She let them know that she was taking on the house-cleanout herself by hiring cleaners and movers. She also told them they would be on the hook financially for their share of the cost.

Annie could not let this stand. "I drove over to her house, and on the way, I had to remind myself that this was not about fighting with my controlling sister; this was about what was best for my parents, who did not want strangers going through their things and deciding what to keep and what to toss. I knew I had to center myself in love for my sister and my family, but I also had to get my point across."

Annie suggested to Debbie that instead of hiring someone for the job, that all of the siblings share calendars online to determine who was available when. She even suggested that Debbie create a timeline with an end date, which would give her the sense of control she needed to have. In the end, the siblings were able to formulate a plan and they are all still speaking, which Annie thinks is a miracle in and of itself!

I understand that acceptance is often easier said than done, especially when you're dealing with a cantankerous boss, a critical parent, or a pain-in-the-rear neighbor. But when you're able to achieve a peaceful union with anyone and everyone, that's when you know you're on the right track. Find something—anything—to help you understand why this person is the way he or she is, and that may also help you to feel compassion for that person's behavior. (For more on compassion and the law of attraction, read Chapter 7.)

Breaking Old Patterns

In order to love our fellow human, we have to let go of issues we have carried with us for years. Hanging on to a grudge isn't loving your fellow human … and, in fact, is only hurting you and affecting the energy *you* send out to (and get back from) the universe. So, by finding something to love about your neighbor, you're showing love for yourself.

Jealousy and anger because someone has more than you are also not loving your fellow human. If you are happy for someone who has more, more will come to you. If you have ill thoughts about someone whom you feel doesn't deserve what he or she has, you are focusing on that situation instead of focusing on your own wants. As you read through this book, you will see that giving attention to negative causes does you no good. So, switch your thoughts to your happy future and stop focusing on those who may have done you wrong (or who just plain annoy the heck out of you).

The Law of Gratitude

Cicero, Roman statesman, orator, and philosopher, said, "Gratitude is not only the greatest of virtues, but the parent of all the others." How right he was!

We all have a list of things we want to come into our lives. Some people want a better job; others want better relationships with their loved ones; some folks want to feel healthier. We think that when we finally have these things, we'll be happy and grateful for them. But there's something missing from this equation—and that's gratitude for the things we have *right now*.

Focusing your gratitude only on the things that are to come has an unintended consequence: you send a negative, ungrateful vibe about the things you already have. So, no matter how much you want change in your life, you have to give thanks for what already is. For example, if you focus on getting a better-paying job while thinking how happy you'll be when you can leave the dump you're working in, you're sending conflicting energies to the universe. Instead, find something—anything—to be grateful for concerning the job you already have, whether it's the fact that it gives you gas money or allows you to interact with all sorts of different people.

Our perspective on life has a lot to do with our future. So, being grateful is powerful, as we are thinking about the good things we have and aren't focusing on what we don't have. In Chapter 5, you'll read about emotion and how it affects what you attract. Thoughts tainted with negative emotion bring more negativity into your life. To help prevent this, take a few minutes every day and come up with at least five things you are grateful for, even if they seem silly. For example ...

> I am grateful I woke up this morning.
>
> I am grateful I have food to eat today and water to drink.
>
> I am grateful I have a job that pays my bills.
>
> I am grateful I have feet and a brain that will take me job hunting.
>
> I am grateful for the power of positive thinking.

Keep doing this, and watch what happens. When you show appreciation for even the most minor things in life, you will be given more of the things you appreciate in life. And because positive thought invades and takes over negative thought patterns, soon you'll find more and more things to be grateful for, which in turn will also come back to you!

The Law of Cause and Effect

Actions and reactions are what the law of cause and effect is about. You do something and you get a reaction based on what you did. You kick a dog and the dog bites you.

Let's hear it for the dog! He doesn't need to be treated that way. He is just being a dog, and that's what dogs do when you're mean to them. But give the pooch hugs and pet him gently, and he'll be wagging his tail and licking your face in no time. Yuck, but still, he does it because of love. Remember, he's just being a dog reacting to the way you treat him.

As a human, you know what you're doing, and you do have a little more control. Energy moves in somewhat of a circular motion. You do something and it eventually comes back around to you. Marketing researcher and director John Richelsen once said,

> Any man will usually get from other men just what he is expecting of them. If he is looking for friendship, he will likely receive it. If his attitude is that of indifference, it will beget indifference. And if a man is looking for a fight, he will in all likelihood be accommodated in that.

Again, this is not a new concept. People have been warning each other about the power of the law of cause and effect for centuries. You probably have heard these sayings:

"How would you like that if someone did that to you?"

"It will come back to you threefold."

"What goes around comes around."

"An eye for an eye; a tooth for a tooth."

"You reap what you sow."

So, this law tells us that every action creates a reaction whether we know it or not. The dog example is pretty straightforward and immediate. Dogs aren't all that complex. Love them and they usually love you back. Hurt them and they'll tear your arm off (or at least try to).

But what happens with the law of cause and effect where human beings are concerned? Heaven knows that with our ulterior motives and twisted thought patterns, nothing is easy!

Monica Needs, Winston Wants—Cause and Effect

As an example of cause and effect, let's look at a relationship situation.

My dear friends Monica and Winston have been together for many years. Several years ago, they had their first child and then another the following year and then a third a couple of years after that. Monica quit her job to stay home with the kids. This was a time in life that she had looked forward to for a long time, and she wanted to be able to completely focus on her family.

Monica really looked forward to her husband, Winston, coming home from work each evening. She truly enjoyed his company, plus she was looking forward to having a break from the kids, if only for 30 minutes or so. She and Winston had always had a very close relationship, and she expected this to be a harried but exciting time of life. And as far as the law of attraction goes, she was doing great! She was focusing on the things she wanted for her future, which included a happy home life.

Well, Monica got the harried part of her vision right. Winston arrived home from work, tired from his long day and not looking forward to dealing with three small children and a needy wife (his words). It wasn't that he wanted them to go away; he just wanted them to be *easier*. As far as the law of attraction is concerned, he was focusing on the things he didn't want in his life at the moment: changing diapers, talking about diapers, and going to the store to buy diapers.

Despite the fact that Winston was not a fully participating partner, Monica kept her focus on a happy family life, and that's what she created. She and the kids were content and comfortable together; Winston kept himself on the outskirts. The more Monica focused on happy family time, the more Winston pulled away, creating his own little bubble.

So ... what are we left with here?

♦ Monica's focus was on the family. Her focus was charged with positive emotion.

♦ Winston's focus was on how he wanted his family to change. Even though this isn't in and of itself a negative thing, his emotions were negative.

♦ Both got what they wanted through the law of cause and effect: Monica achieved a secure family base (minus Winston), while Winston got a family that was easy to deal with because they hardly interacted with him.

Now this may not seem like the happiest outcome, but that depends on your definition of happiness. Winston's focus on having his own life was so strong that Monica could not simply overcome it with her own desires, so she reangled her request to include situations over which she would have some measure of control. (In Chapter 13, you'll read more about frustrating relationships and what the law of attraction can—and can't—do about them.)

Is this an example of "what goes around comes around"? I think so. Winston kept his distance from his family, and now they keep their distance from him. Sad, yes, but a good example of the law of cause and effect in everyday life.

Karma

What we do in one lifetime dictates what happens to us in another. That's also a type of cause and effect and it's called *karma*, which originated in the Hindu religion but has since been adapted by other spiritual traditions as well. The theory goes that if we're kind and good to people and have a positive energy in this lifetime, we may come back in an elevated life-form next time around. If we're mean and rotten and surrounded by negative vibes throughout this lifetime, we may come back in a "demoted" life-form. The whole point of karma is to teach us the things we need to learn about, so we can one day reach nirvana, or paradise, where we won't incarnate again.

There are those who believe that karma is what makes up our personalities, our wisdom, and our likes and dislikes of things that we experience in our present existence on planet Earth. There are also other philosophies that subscribe to similar beliefs. (Namely, that what we've done in past lives influences where we are and what we do in our current lives.) Whether you believe this is not the point; hundreds of millions of people do. They live their lives according to the law of cause and effect, hoping to do better the next time around.

Acting with Intent

It's one thing to act and react. That's human nature. But when you do something with the intent to hurt, destroy, trick, or take away from another, that's about being selfish.

There is so much for everyone on this planet, we have no reason to try to take away from one another or intentionally make someone unhappy. Intentionally creating a situation that hurts someone else is not going to get you anywhere. The universe is a circle, constantly moving, flowing, and redepositing the energy it receives. So, whatever you launch out there will eventually fall back on you with all the gusto it took for you to send it out in the first place.

When you are in a competition and you think, "I want to win and I want Bill to lose," that's not really being evil or bad—as long as you haven't tampered with Bill's chances of winning! That's just part of the fun of the sport. But sitting and focusing your nasty thoughts on someone else is harmful, if not to them, then to you and the energy you send out.

It's easy to sit around and wish bad things for other people; it's even relatively easy to cook up some plot to hurt them. However, it is work to take the focus off the people you dislike and to put it on yourself—on the things you want in your life—and to take the time to rework your thought patterns and ask the universe for help. It's time consuming. And it's even scary because you have to take a good look at your life and decide what's working and what isn't. (If you're focusing all of that negative energy on someone else, I can tell you that there is definitely something that isn't working!)

Lose the anger; focus on yourself. You'll note that there's no law that says you have to stay stuck in the same situation forever. Use the tools here to help you break free of old patterns and move on.

CHAPTER 3

Key Elements of Attraction

No matter what you read or how many different people you talk to about the law of attraction, it always comes down to these three key elements: asking, believing, and receiving. These do not change, even if the methods for accessing them do.

"Sounds pretty easy," you say. "So, I ask, I believe, and I receive the benefits into my life. Consider it done!" In theory, it does sound simple. But in application, it requires training yourself to have a complete understanding of these key elements and their purposes. Once you have that comprehension, you can start plugging into these principles whenever you need to and using the law of attraction to your benefit.

Because we'll be talking about these concepts repeatedly throughout the book, I'll give you an overview of them in this chapter. Keep in mind as you read that one element cannot stand alone: all three must work together.

Ask for What You Want

The first process of fulfilling any objective is deciding what you want and then asking for it. By the process of elimination you can get a better idea of what your aspirations are. We'll talk about evaluating and weeding out requests in more detail in Chapter 9. It's basically sorting out what you want from what you don't want and putting your positive energy into that want list.

Your thoughts are like a snowball on a hill. The more you roll that ball of snow, the larger it becomes. Likewise, the more thought you give to a certain desire, the stronger it becomes, and the law of attraction starts listening. But when you think about what you don't want, you are also giving attention to that, and the law of attraction starts noticing. You want to make sure you're attracting the right things, and it all starts in the way you ask for them.

Not the World Wide Web—the Universal Web

The attraction principle picks up the keywords you focus on and sends what you asked for back to you. It's a little like typing keywords into a search engine on your computer. Let's say you're looking for a flat-screen television. If you type in keywords like *flat screen, free shipping,* and, *no old-fashioned big-tube televisions,* your results will most likely give you places to purchase flat-screen televisions with free shipping and places that charge shipping fees; additionally you will receive information about places where you can purchase old-fashioned televisions with big tubes.

So, why are you not getting the perfect search results? The search system often disregards the word *no*. Type in "chocolate cake with no nuts", and guess what? You will get recipes for cakes both with and without nuts. You might also get brownie recipes with no nuts, but … wait a minute, you wanted cake! You can see how "nuts" this can be if you don't know how to direct your thoughts about what you want and how to make requests.

So, when you ask for a job that doesn't make you miserable, guess what? The universe hears *job* and *miserable*. When you say, "I don't want a man I have to support," guess what kind of boyfriend you're going to end up with?

Think about this: the "wants" always win. I *want* my readers to understand what I am explaining. The universe will translate this request like so: readers, understand, explanation. Now I could have phrased that request as, "I don't want my readers to get confused." The universe's translation of that: readers ... confused. Oh my!

Right now, try to get "I don't want" out of your thought patterns. You need not regulate every single thought, but slowly try to catch yourself and think in terms of what you *want*. After a while, it becomes a habit. I'll touch on this concept in more detail in following chapters.

Loud and Clear!

If you send requests for what you *think* you want, but in your heart you are not 100 percent sure, you will get unclear results. For example, a thought such as "I want to find a job where I only work mornings ... but if the days were only Tuesdays and Thursdays, I guess I could work afternoons, too," is chock-full of mixed vibrations. You can't expect an ideal work schedule to materialize if you're not even certain what your idea of ideal is!

Maybe you're thinking about your life in general, such as "I want a home on the water—a lake or the ocean—but I do like the mountains, so it doesn't matter. I guess I could do either." Then you continue "I also want children, maybe two, maybe three. A job in the city would be pretty nice, unless I find a job in a trendy small town with a sophisticated attitude." While it's nice to be open-minded, the vibrations of these thoughts are all over the place! They aren't the least bit focused; they're like a weak radio signal. The universe might receive the station but with lots of static. When you listen to a station with bad reception, you don't always catch every word, and the information *you* end up with could bear little resemblance to what was actually said. Now imagine the universe receiving bits and pieces of your messages—eek!

How would you rephrase this all-over-the-map request? First, decide what you really want, then tell the universe—and don't be shy! Clear your mind and focus on your request: "I want a house on Cape Cod with a view of the ocean. I also want to find a job that allows me to work from home because I want to have two children, one boy and one girl, within the next five years."

Don't ask until you're clear. By asking with intention, direction, and the knowledge that if you ask, you will receive it, you launch a strong vibration of desire. Nothing will be lost in translation, in other words.

Become a Believer

"Knock and the door shall be open." "Ask and it shall be given." These are just a couple of quotes which make the point that the law of attraction will give you what you want if you ask, believe, and receive. Now that you've learned how to ask for what you want, you just need to believe it's possible, and let the universe do the rest. This sounds pretty easy, but I assure you, for many people—especially those who are real go-getters—having faith that the universe will respond to your request in due time is the most difficult part.

Step Back

My best advice is that you don't attempt to contemplate how your request is going to come to fruition, but know in your heart that it will be so. The biggest part is you must really *feel* that your request will come to fruition.

Because of past experiences, it's easy to think you know what to expect, so you believe the outcome of any given situation is already set in stone. You're not believing in the possibilities of the universe.

Now, of course, there are some physical situations that tend to produce the same results, time and time again. You figured out a long time ago that if you jump up, you will come right back down to the ground; if you stick your hand in fire, you will get burned; if you put your lips to an ice cube, they will stick. You have accepted these outcomes as truth. You have no doubt that standing in the rain will result in soaked clothing. Now, try having that kind of faith in the universe.

Here's the deal: you have to let go and just believe. Start with small, simple requests that aren't going to make or break your life, like "I want my plants to survive." I know, it sounds silly, but this is the kind of request that's easy for you to focus on initially—and more importantly, it's easy for you to let the universe have control in this situation. This is like a training session for your mind. Once the law of attraction starts to work for you in simpler areas of your life, believing becomes easier. So, send out your request and let your higher power, God, or *source* (which refers to the nonphysical root of all things in the universe and the power or presence that resides over everything) do its job.

Know It Will Come

By nature, we have a tendency to try to figure out or to understand how things are going to work out. If you were to borrow money from someone, for example, you might wonder if she has it already available in cash, or if she has to change over funds from one account to another, or whether she herself will have to borrow it, or if she will need to take it out of a credit card, and so on. The reality is if she said she would loan you the money, it doesn't matter how she gets it (as long as it's legal, of course).

Some people try to figure out the way people and things function more than others. A person who always wants to know how things operate may spend a lot of valuable time contemplating such things when it really doesn't matter!

My neighbor, for instance, hired someone to trim his very large oak trees. He was very concerned about how the tree trimmer was going to do this: Would he use a ladder, would he climb the tree, or would he use some type of a lift? How would he then haul the branches away? Would he bring a truck, would he have some type of dumpster, or would he hire outside contractors for the disposal? As I stood there in amazement (thinking "I can use this story for my book"), I finally had to say, "Let's talk about something else. You hired him for the job, he's worked for you before, and the job always gets done, so don't worry about the details of how it's going to happen." His response was, "But if I don't worry about how it's going to get done, who will?"

In this case, the tree trimmer had all the answers, the job was completed perfectly, and all the worry my neighbor invested in the project turned out to be useless. Had my neighbor approached the tree trimmer with all of his worries and muddied the waters, so to speak, the job might not have turned out as well—just like when we send mixed signals to the universe.

You also hinder the vibration when you use words like can't and don't. We have thoughts like this every day without even realizing it. It isn't necessary to know *how* you will end up with your heart's desire, just know that it *will* come to you.

I sit here at my computer typing away, and I have no idea how it technically works. All I know is that I turn it on and start to type, and away I go. I am the same way with my hot rollers. I plug them in, they heat up, I roll them into my hair, I take them out after 10 minutes, and I have wavy hair. I follow the process, and I achieve my goal without needing to know the mechanics behind it. The art of believing isn't so different. You have to accept it will happen and just wait for the result to come into your life without fighting or questioning it.

Receive without Reservation

Because now you are consciously aware of the three key elements of the law of attraction, even if you may only be pondering these concepts, you are that much closer to achieving your goals. You have asked, you have believed, and now it's time for the finale: you have to receive (or allow) what you are attempting to attract.

Try to feel the magic of having what you want. Do some daydreaming. If you finally got rid of those allergies you've had for years, would your life change because you could finally walk in the woods? If your significant other finally comes around to your point of view on your shared finances, how would that feel? Suppose you got a call inviting you to interview for your dream job; how would that affect your outlook on life? And how about if that sports car you've had your eye on is marked down to a close-out price that you can actually afford?

The reason I advise doing some daydreaming about these matters is not because I want you to waste time. It's because it's one thing to say, "I know that this is what I want," and it's quite another to put yourself in the reality of that situation. But that's what you have to do in order to know if it's something that you're willing to receive. For example, let's say you land an interview for your dream job. As you prepare to wow your potential employer, you begin to think, "What will this job do to my relationship? Will my husband be threatened because I'll earn more than he does? I'll have to travel a lot. Can we adjust, or will it be the end of our marriage?" I'd bet dollars to doughnuts that your interview is not going to go very well because you're not sure that you can handle such a major change in your life. In order to receive, you *have* to feel joy and happiness about what you're asking for; doubt is negative energy and brings about negative results.

The happiness you feel is like a flag waving down the goal you are trying to achieve. You have asked, you believed, and now the receiving is the flag signaling that vibration back to you. "Yoo-hoo! Here I am, and I want you to come to me."

Here are some exercises to incorporate into your requests:

- Give thanks to the universe, God, or whichever higher source you subscribe to for bringing your requests into your life. Do this before you even receive them. Your gratitude is positive energy, which reinforces your request and belief.
- Take a few minutes every day to think about your goal or desires and feel the happiness of that situation. This not only gives your request a boost, but it also reinforces your belief.

It doesn't matter who you are thanking (God, the universe, or source), as long as you understand there is something going on out there that is beyond what you can fathom and it's bringing about what you desire.

PART 2

Can You Feel It?

When it comes to asking anything of the universe, if you don't feel it, then it's not coming to you anytime soon. Emotion plays an important part in your requests. Learning to use positive feelings to underscore your desires helps to bring those things into your life smoothly and easily. Hanging on to negative emotions, on the other hand, is a surefire way to sabotage yourself. In these chapters, you'll read about the ways your thoughts may already be helping—or hindering—your intent.

CHAPTER 4

Think About It, Bring It About

What comes to mind when you hear someone described as having a magnetic personality? Most people tend to think of those who have a whole lot of charisma and a special knack for drawing others to them. But this terminology can actually be used to describe everyone on the planet because our thoughts draw not only people to us but situations and material things, too. Unfortunately, we don't always attract what we would describe as good people, places, and things—but each one of us has the ability to change that.

In Part 1, I explained how you've produced your state of mind, your job, and your financial status, perhaps without being aware of doing so. Now, here comes the big question: if you are not aware of how you cocreated your current situation, how can you change it?

You're a Package Deal

Take this book and walk over to your mirror. Believe it or not, you're not only gazing upon a reflection of your face, but you're also seeing the entirety of your existence. That's right: when you peer into the mirror, you're looking at your career, your education, your friends, your possessions, and everything else in your life. You've created your entire life package using your own thoughts.

As you read in Chapter 1, every thought is a vibration. When you think something, whether the thought is positive or negative, you're inviting it into your life and creating it. You are like a transmitter sending out signals to the universe, telling it what to give back to you. So, if the person staring back at you in the looking glass is a successful and happy person, congratulations! You transmitted positive vibrations and they've come back to you. But if you're staring at someone in the mirror who looks a bit worn out and not very happy ... oops! You sent out the wrong signals. And negative signals can be every bit as detrimental to your physical well-being as your emotional state.

Positive Pound Loss

Let's look at weight gain as an example of the law of attraction. Let's say you have been dieting all week and then comes the moment of truth when you step on the scale. You look down, see your weight, get off the scale, kick it, and say, "Oh, no! I will never lose weight. I've gained 4 pounds!" In response to your negative vibrations, the universe says, "Okey dokey, I'll make it so. You will never lose weight and will continue to gain more. Now what else do you want?"

Not content to stop there, you think to yourself, "That lousy diet food doesn't work. I wasted my money." The universe says, "All righty, that diet food doesn't work and you wasted your money. Anything else you want to vibrate into your life to make yourself unhappy and overweight?"

Last, you think, "I'll never get in a relationship while I'm this heavy." I think you know what happens next.

Could this situation end on a more positive note, with hope and not despair as its outcome? Of course it can—but that's up to you. Just as you attract all things in life, you can also deflect those extra pounds—or anything else you don't want—by using your energy in the right way. Focus your positive energy by saying, "Nothing is impossible. I have to continue to treat my body well and provide it with a healthful diet and exercise, and I *know* I'll lose the weight."

I'll leave you with a quote from Walter Anderson, founder and author of *The Confidence Course*: "You and I are not what we eat; we are what we think." This works on so many levels! For one thing, it speaks to our mind-set as it relates to weight. Being thin doesn't make us "good" and being heavy doesn't make us "bad." For another, it speaks to what we bring about in our lives—health, appearance, and relationships. Ultimately, it's not about what we put into our mouths—it's about what we allow into our minds!

Blaming Makes Things Worse

We tend to blame other people or circumstances for making our lives miserable. Surely, if we were in total control of our lives, none of us would have to deal with cranky bosses, irritating family members, low-paying jobs, or health issues. Well, guess what? Each one of us *is* in total control. We all have to come to terms with the idea that we've cocreated (with the universal energy) our state of affairs and being. So, drop thoughts such as, "If I hadn't had five children, I would be wealthy today," or, "I'd be happier if my coworkers weren't so dumb." And please stop blaming your parents, whether they're alive or dead, for your own grown-up miseries. (My mother thanked me for including this sentence.)

Negative thoughts about people bring about more and more negative circumstances, especially when you're so focused on the behavior of others that you forget to focus on *your* wants. Make a conscious effort not to play the blame game anymore, even though it can feel *soooo* good sometimes. You're truly only hurting yourself with the negative vibrations these kinds of thoughts attract.

Rise and Whine?

Do you know that you can wake up in the morning and decide whether or not your day will go well? It's that whole getting-up-on-the-wrong-side-of-the-bed theory. If you believe your day is going down the tubes from the moment your alarm clock blares, the universe will make sure to match your expectations, point for point.

Down the Drain

Let's use Arlene, a physical therapist, as an example of negative energy feeding on itself. Arlene woke up the other morning in a good mood. (So far, so good—she got up on the *right* side of the bed, so to speak.) But while she was getting ready for work, she dropped her diamond earring down the bathroom sink. Instantly, her mind went to the negative: "This is all I need. I'm going to be late for work. I can't afford another set of diamond earrings. I'll never get it out of there. This day is off to a horrible start!"

In her negative state of mind, she ripped her new blouse as she pulled it on. "This is going to be one of those days," she said to herself (and the universe). "Everything is already going wrong and it's only 7:15. I can imagine what's going to happen at work!" Then she went back to the sink—her mind filled with negativity about the upcoming day—forgot about the earring in the drainpipe, and turned on the water. Bye-bye, earring.

They say that good things come to those who wait. Well, bad things come to those who expect them. Naturally, Arlene was creating more negativity. She was unconsciously asking the universe to bring in more and more negative events … and she got her wish!

Stop in Your Tracks!

You've no doubt had days that started out badly and only got worse, but perhaps you never stopped to think about your responsibility in all of the drama. Maybe on some particularly bad days, you've really believed that you were the victim of fate or bad luck. Well, you were really the victim of your own negative energy. You can't expect the universe to weave a beautiful day for you if all you're providing is garbage for it to work with. So, how can you stop yourself before the bad vibes start spinning out of control?

Let's go back to Arlene. When she dropped her earring down the sink, she should have stopped and focused for a minute. Then she should have thought, "I can't get my earring back by myself, so I'll have to call a plumber later. My earring isn't going anywhere for now, so I won't worry about it. I want to have a good day, so I have to leave this behind for right now." (Notice how she focuses on what she *wants* instead of what she doesn't want—more about that in the next section.) Her positive vibes would have helped to calm her, she probably wouldn't have torn her blouse, and she most likely would not have flushed her earring down the drain to its ultimate demise.

No matter how badly your day, week, month, or year is going, you can start turning it around right now. Stop negative thoughts in their tracks and refuse to think that way anymore. Focus on what you want to change, and before you know it, things will start improving.

Want vs. Don't Want

In a nutshell, staying positive will help you send out a vibration that will bring positive things back to you. There's a definite method to keeping your thoughts on the positive side. You may have to practice it a bit, but after a while it will come naturally.

Here's the secret: you want to concentrate on what you want as opposed to what you don't want. I know it sounds like splitting hairs, but there's a big difference in the type of vibration you send out with each of these types of thoughts. When you focus on what you don't want, that negative attention in and of itself will bring it to you. You move in the direction that dominates your mind, so prevent the "don'ts" from taking over your thoughts. You're working with a source that understands what you are thinking about most and sends it to you.

Here are a few examples of how to change the negative energy of "don't want" to the positive vibration of "want":

> *Think:* I want to keep my job.
> *Not:* I don't want to get fired.

> *Think:* I want to get into a healthy relationship.
> *Not:* I don't want a dysfunctional mate.

> *Think:* I want to have financial security.
> *Not:* I don't want to always have bills I can't pay.

> *Think:* I want to be healthy.
> *Not:* I don't want to get sick.

Start practicing this method of positive thinking right now, and try to catch yourself when you find you're concentrating on what you don't want. Keep a journal or list of the negative thoughts you have each day and find a way to "rethink" them. It takes some time to rewire your thought process, but in the end, it will become second nature. At that point, you'll experience a change in what you're attracting to your life.

Don't Worry (Much)

Sometimes worry itself can create the things in life we don't want to happen. Worry sends out such a powerful negative signal to the universe, it's like throwing a rubber ball at the wall at 80 mph. There's just no doubt that it's going to come right back and hit you in the head.

I'm not suggesting that everyone should ignore the impulse to feel anxious in certain situations. Worry is what protects us from danger and can actually be useful at times. It's when worry serves no useful purpose that it becomes harmful.

Let's say you live in New York and have a very important job interview in Massachusetts on Friday. Starting Monday, all you can think about is that meeting. If you focus on positive thoughts ("I'm going to do well; the trip will be a breeze; nothing bad is going to happen") you're home free, but when that demon worry starts creeping in, you're setting yourself up for hard times.

So, on Monday, you may be excited about that job interview … but then you start thinking, "It will take me two hours to get there by train. What if the train is late? Oh geez, I hope it won't be late. And if it snows and they have to clear the tracks, that could delay me even more. I just hope I'm not late because of that stupid train. My girlfriend's train was an hour late last week. That could very easily happen to me."

Then you decide to buy your ticket in advance. When you get your ticket you immediately think, "I'd better not lose this because if there's a line at the station on Friday, I might not be able to get another one. Or what if I forget my wallet, and I can't pay for another one? Oh boy, maybe this whole thing is a waste of time. I think a lot more people will be more qualified than me, and they probably won't be taking a train to the interview because they *know* trains can be late!"

I Knew It!

So, what are you doing here? You are putting out a very strong set of signals to the universe—"Train will be late; interview will go badly; I won't get the job"—and are actually attracting trouble. Of course, Friday rolls around and your train is late. (See how powerful you are, and you didn't even know it!) You don't get the job, and you're really not surprised … because you "knew" all along that this would happen.

Now stop and think of a time you did this sort of thing to yourself. Consider how things could have worked out differently if you'd "known" that everything was going to go smoothly.

Prescription for Anti-Pessimism

No one is expecting you to be all smiles 24 hours a day, but if you are a worrier, acknowledge what those negative thoughts are bringing into your life. And *please* don't say things like, "I just can't help it, I tend to worry." You're not fooling the universe by offering up an excuse for your state of mind; you're only creating more worry and more negative vibrations!

One woman, whom we'll call Stacy, set herself up for big-time life issues simply by believing she was ill. She invested all of her energy into thinking she was dying, even though doctor after doctor told her that she wasn't. She was living her life in a constant state of panic, always worried about what *might* happen. What if her husband left her because of her "illness"? Would her friends be up to the challenge of supporting her during her dying days? How would her boss handle having a terminally ill woman in the office? Well, guess what happened to Stacy? Her career took a nosedive, her friends dropped out of sight, and her husband became distant.

Stacy eventually worked herself out of her hypochondria with the power of positive thoughts. "I refused to invest any more time or energy into thinking about scary things that *could* happen. Now I try to focus on the possibilities that life has to offer and I find that everything else just falls into place."

That's some sage advice from a woman who's seen both sides of the positive/negative-vibe coin.

Some people have taken worry to such heightened levels that they have developed what is described by professionals as Generalized Anxiety Disorder (GAD). This state of mind is characterized by disproportionate and senseless worry that lasts approximately six months or more. If you feel like you need professional help dealing with worry, contact your primary doctor for guidance.

Congratulations ... I Hate You

It's important to recognize how you generally think about others. We all want to better ourselves and have peaceful, harmonious, healthy, and financially stable lives, but it worries me when I hear people say they are jealous of those who have found that balance. Being envious of those who "have" and feeling like you're a "have-not" only makes matters worse.

Negative-minded people are great at focusing on what other people are up to. When you say things like, "She always does better than I do," you are actually helping that other person to *do* better than you. Remember: the universe is giving you what you want, so if you truly believe that someone is better than you are, you're fueling her success with your thoughts about her.

Don't get me wrong. There's nothing wrong with wishing people well, but there's obviously a big difference between wishing for the best for someone and being envious of someone whom you believe doesn't deserve what he or she has. Here's the kicker: when you think you're venting about someone who is "favored by the gods" (someone who was born with a silver spoon in his mouth or someone who has way more success than you believe he deserves), you are helping to create more success for him! Meanwhile, you're keeping yourself in a holding pattern with the other person always doing better than you.

How do you break this pattern, especially when the other person seems to have so much power over you and other people? Simple. Acknowledge that there's enough happiness and success to go around. One person doesn't get to have all of it, in other words, and you don't have to fear that he's taking your share of good things. Don't begrudge the other person his triumphs; just say to yourself, "He's done well. But I know I can do as well or even better!"

Stop thinking of other people as thorns in your side. You can become just as happy and successful as they are by investing your passion in the power of positive thoughts. Believe that you really are deserving and that you merit good things in life, and the things you crave will be only a thought away.

From Thought to Words to Reality

I cannot reiterate enough how your thoughts should focus on confident thinking. If you can stop yourself from saying things like "with my luck ..." you'll move closer to a more desirable life. Luck has nothing to do with it. It would be more accurate for you to say, "With my negative thinking and the tense vibrations I'm sending out to the universe, the only things that *can* happen to me today will be negative."

The more you understand the law of attraction, the more you can focus on using your intent to better your life. Lending your attention or thought to something (positive or negative) is as good as giving it an engraved invitation to enter your life. And it doesn't matter if you keep your thoughts to yourself. The universe is omnipotent—you just can't pull a fast one over on it, no matter how clever you think you are.

So, whether you speak out loud about your desires or say them in your mind, the laws of attraction are the same. In other words, your vibration doesn't need a physical voice in order to be heard. It's out there—and the universe is receiving it loud and clear!

Although every thought is a transmission to the universe, you don't have to live in fear every second of the day. For goodness' sake, your mind is working all the time; if you had to edit each and every thought, you'd never get through your day! So, even though you are always sending out messages to the universal source, the ones that are heard most clearly are boosted by emotion and intention.

In other words, don't panic if you have a thought that isn't 100 percent positive or if you happen to say something that sounds negative. Saying, "You're bad!" to your friend while she's sharing a funny story and you're cracking up is far different than yelling the same thing to someone who's just stepped on your lawn. Similarly, singing your favorite blues song isn't necessarily going to make you blue, and send out a negative vibe to the universe. Don't live in fear of your thoughts and words— just make sure to back them up with positive passion.

You're only starting to plant good thoughts. It takes lots of attention to make them grow. Throughout the remainder of the book, I'll provide you with more methods for turning negative vibes into positive life changes.

CHAPTER 5

No Emotion, No Attraction

Let's step this learning up a notch with a little extra emotion or feeling so your request is initiated with a bigger boost of vibrations. The energy you send out to the universe has to be strong and clear in order for it to be answered—and I'm talking about positive energy as well as negative energy.

Now don't start obsessing over every single idea that goes through your mind. One passing negative thought isn't going to get you in the doghouse with the universe, nor will one fleeting positive thought bring you wondrous things. It's when your thoughts are backed with strong, *consistent* emotion that the universe really starts to listen.

Primer for Your Mind

When I talk about the emotional part of the law of attraction, I mean the feeling you get when you make a decision about what it is you desire in life. When you ask for something, your mind should be clear of any other thoughts, and you have to feel that what you seek is what you definitely want.

In other words, there are to be no distractions, no multitasking (asking of the universe while simultaneously texting a friend will put you way behind in this process), no wishy-washy requests, and no hemming and hawing while asking something of the universe. That is, unless you want a response that's somewhat off the mark!

Learn to Be Stern

You have to be a little tough on yourself to shift into a vibration that is going to bring you what you want. Don't focus your thoughts on past negative experiences. In doing so, you are giving attention to them. And because negative emotion attracts a negative response, you're shooting yourself in the foot. Antoine de Saint-Exupéry said, "The important thing is to strive toward a goal that is not immediately visible. That goal is not the concern of the mind but of the spirit." This can be difficult, but that's what makes it worth the effort!

If your request goes something like "I wish I could find a nice boyfriend. I've wasted so much time dating terrible men. I just want my rotten life to improve," then you're infusing your request with negative energy from past experiences.

It's hard to break these patterns of negative thought once they've firmly taken root in your head. But if you want positive results, you have to start out with positive intent—and don't allow yourself to waver from this stance, no matter how dire the circumstances! So, in this example, you might say something like "I want to find a nice boyfriend. I deserve one; I'm ready for one, and I want to move forward into a better life." See the difference? Not only are you using positive language here, but you're also focusing on a brighter *future*.

Lose the Negative Excitability

When you ask anything of the universe, you should feel a sense of excitement and yearning in a positive way, as opposed to focusing on the lack of love, money, friendships, etc. in your life. Experience the happiness of what you know is coming to you.

Here's an easy example to illustrate this point: imagine you're buying a new house in a better neighborhood, but all you can think about is how happy you are to be moving away from those neighbors you never liked, and how your old house had no dishwasher, a leaky roof, and no backyard. That's pure negative emotion. When you get to your new place, you'll think of it as an escape—not a destination.

On the other hand, if you take the time to think about the excitement of being in a new home and all the joy you're bound to experience there, your mind is steeping itself in the positive possibilities that lie ahead. Negative emotions will only bring you negative circumstances.

Thinking clear and precise thoughts, feeling the bliss of what they will bring, and allowing them to come into your life will bring around your desires specifically and easily. It's like a boomerang. You send out the vibration and it comes back to you. Weak vibrations come back with faulty results. Strong vibrations come back with vigor.

What Goes Around Comes Around

When most people use the expression "what goes around comes around," they typically mean that if you do something mean-spirited, you'll get something negative back from the universe. But if you strive to do good things, you'll experience goodness in your life.

As far as attracting positive things into your life goes, I don't believe that doing good deeds is sufficient if you're not emotionally invested in your actions. Let's say that you're taking care of an elderly relative. Your friends and neighbors look at you and say, "Wow, Sally is so good and kind to take in her grandfather like that. She deserves good things in life." The twist to the story is that you are not helping Grandpa out of the goodness of your heart; you're doing it because you expect your parents to send you a caretaker's fee, and you also think that you're setting yourself up pretty nicely for an inheritance when Grandpa passes on.

Ooooh, big difference between the two. You might fool your pals, but you're not fooling the universe. The universe sends back the same type of energy that you invest in your dealings with other people. If you're a kind soul, that's great news. But if you're trafficking in sneaky, underhanded doings ... well, what goes around comes around!

Decide It, Believe It, Expect It

Before you can expect the law of attraction to work for you, you have to make a firm decision to believe that it *will* work. In other words, you have to make an emotional investment in your request. There's that old saying, "Nothing ventured, nothing gained." That pretty well sums up the law of attraction, at least as far as your emotions go.

Once you ask anything of the universe, you have to believe or feel it will happen—and you have to really want it. If you don't truly and from every fiber of your being believe in it, then you are delaying things, at best, and possibly even totally negating them. It's scary to invest your hopes and dreams into something you want so badly, but I assure you that without that level of commitment, your circumstances won't change (at least not for the better).

False Hopes Keep You Hoping

Dale Carnegie, the famed author and self-improvement expert, once said, "When dealing with people, remember: you are not dealing with creatures of logic but creatures of emotion." This is good and bad news as far as the law of attraction goes!

When we use the law of attraction, there are no limits, but without emotion and belief, you'll be left holding a bag of false hopes. We all know what false hopes are. It's like looking at the size 4 dress you bought to wear at your class reunion two months ago because you said you were going to lose 20 pounds. And here you sit with one last day to diet, and you haven't lost an ounce. False hope in this case sounds a little like, "Well, maybe I will wake up tomorrow morning 20 pounds thinner." Yeah, right.

You didn't invest your time, energy, and attention into losing that weight, which is why you'll be wearing an old outfit to your reunion. The law of attraction also requires your time, energy, and attention. If you fail to feed your requests with positive emotion and belief, you'll be stuck in the same old ruts, wondering why nothing is changing for you.

And that's the false hope—that just because you send it out to the universe, your request should come barreling right back to you. It doesn't work that way. I think the least you can do to achieve your goal is to put a little emotional effort into it, don't you?

Test It Out

Sometimes it's good to start out with small requests that are fairly easy to invest your emotions in. For example, it probably doesn't matter to you one way or the other if you have to wait 10 minutes for a seat in a busy restaurant. But of course, it would be nice not to wait. As you drive to the restaurant, ask the universe to clear out a seat for you. Wrap this in belief and positive emotion, and watch what happens.

Every time we go to a certain restaurant for lunch, my husband and I want a booth. So, before I leave my house, I think and feel that we will get a booth. Ninety-nine percent of the time there is a booth available for us, even when the restaurant is otherwise full.

My husband, unaware that I request this of the universe, says, "It seems that no matter what time we come in here, we always get a booth." Well, I have *two* things working for me here: I have asked, believed, and allowed a booth to come into my life, but my husband (unknowingly) helps by saying, "Wow, we always get a booth!" He believes and expects this will happen, too! He tells his friends, "Every time we go to that restaurant, we get a booth." When we take friends to the same restaurant they repeat it: "It's amazing that you guys always get a booth here." So, now we have even more people rooting for us. You can see how the vibration expands.

So, stop saying, "I never get this," and "I never get that." Make a request of the universe, and then say, "I *know* that this good thing will happen for me." Change the way you think and speak, and positive experiences will enter your life!

I realize that you may have more pressing concerns than getting a good seat for dinner, but this same theory will work for any request once you get that vibe going.

Partner Up with Your Gut Feeling

Your emotions also serve another purpose: they help you determine whether your requests are "right" for you. This is a blessing, in my mind. Your inner self is clear as can be. You should never have to guess if you are doing or asking for the right thing. If your request makes you feel happy and at peace, it's right for you. If it makes you feel uncomfortable, then it's not. It's that simple. (And, when it feels right, plug in those emotions and ask for it!)

You'll hear different terminology for your internal voice. For example, in *The Law of Attraction: The Basics of the Teachings of Abraham*, authors Esther and Jerry Hicks use specific terminology for explaining what your emotions are telling you. They refer to this as an *emotional guidance system*.

For years, I have used this guidance system. If something doesn't feel right, I simply do not ask for it. On the other hand, if everyone thinks what I want is impossible, but it "feels right" to me, I frankly don't care. I expect my requests to come to fruition and they have. I trust my guidance system—and you should trust yours.

Record What You Want (and Why You Want It)

We all have desires that we're unsure of, even when we try to listen to that gut feeling. When that happens, I find it's helpful to break it all down in black and white. Michael Leboeuf, business consultant, speaker, and author said, "When you write down your ideas, you automatically focus your full attention on them. Few if any of us can write one thought and think another at the same time. Thus, a pencil and paper make excellent concentration tools."

I know that writing it all out makes it easier for me to decide where I really stand on a confusing issue. If I feel joy and happiness and have a good, excited feeling in my stomach, I go for it! On the other hand, if I feel unhappy or nervous, I give it a pass.

Keeping a journal of thoughts and desires is easier than you might think. All you need is some sort of notebook. (It doesn't need to be leather bound, or have a lock, or be anything fancy. In fact, you can buy a cheap notebook at a grocery store or keep your entries on your computer or cell phone.) Use this format to help your process:

> I think I want ...
>
> I want this because ...
>
> When I get this, my life will change because ...

When you're done, put your writing away. Come back to it the next day:

> Now that I read this, it makes me feel ...

Then wait a day or two and read it again:

> This is the second time I am reading this, and now I feel ...

Wait a few days more and read it again:

> After reading this for the third time, I now feel ...

Here's an example. I've underlined what you might fill in:

> I think I want <u>a new job</u>.
>
> I want this because <u>I hate my present job, and I am overworked and underpaid</u>.
>
> When I get this, my life will change because <u>I will be making more money, so I will be happier</u>.

On the second day:

> Now that I read this, it makes me feel <u>nervous because I don't know what else is out there, but excited because I could get out of debt.</u>

On the third day:

> This is the second time I am reading this, and now I feel <u>that finding a new job could take a while because I don't know what I want to do yet, so I feel frightened that I might be jumping the gun.</u>

On the fourth day:

> After reading this the third time, I now feel <u>that I'd better rethink this. I am getting a sinking feeling inside.</u>

We often send out vibrations of what we *think* we want too quickly. So, the request gets sent out, you change your mind, and the universe hears all of these conflicting emotions from you. It's no wonder our requests go so horribly awry sometimes! Before you ask for anything, take the time to evaluate whether it's right for you. After all, if it's something you truly want, you have the rest of your life to revel in it. You can wait a few more days before working on bringing it to fruition.

The Mind-Body Connection in Action

As you've already learned, investing your emotion into your requests is an important part of using the law of attraction to your benefit. But it's just as important to invest some physical intent into your request. The law of attraction doesn't work by magic. It works by combining your physical and emotional energies. Asking the universe to let you win at the racetrack won't do you much good if you don't place the bet.

In this section, I'll give you a couple of examples of people who learned the importance of the mind-body connection and went on to achieve their desired goals as a result!

Dennis the Tennis Menace

Dennis, a friend of mine, was a semipro tennis player preparing to compete in a tournament. Dennis had the skills to win; he just fell apart emotionally during the big matches. To his friends' collective surprise, he not only performed well during this tournament, he won it!

Afterward, I said to him, "What a change! You really held yourself together!" He said, "I visualized myself winning this time, and it really worked. I could see the trophy, hear the applause, smell the sweat—everything! I just knew it was going to happen this time!"

Although Dennis didn't call his method the law of attraction, that's exactly what it was. He sent a positive vibration out, he expected to win, and he got exactly what he wanted. He had the talent all along. He just needed to believe.

Mary, Mary, Quite Contrary

My friend Mary said to me, "I'm trying so hard to lose weight. My doctor says that if I don't drop 50 pounds, I'm risking diabetes, high blood pressure, and joint problems." I could tell that she was concerned, but she also added, "I'm ready to do this. I'm going to ask the universe to help me. There's no reason this can't happen."

Well, weeks went by with no change in Mary's weight. Then months went by. Still … nothing. I was getting agitated because I knew Mary had invested positive energy into this request, and she kept telling me, "I know I'm going to lose the weight soon."

You know the ending to this story: although Mary had changed her outlook and believed it was absolutely possible to lose the weight, she hadn't changed her lifestyle one iota. She was still eating too much and not exercising at all. As a result, no results!

Now to be fair, we all know people who try to lose weight while making the necessary adjustments to their lifestyle and *still* don't have much success. Why does *this* happen?

Well, as I said at the beginning of this section, the law of attraction is not some magic trick. It takes some work on your part. Many times, people will diet with a discouraged attitude, never believing that they will slim down. The universe, of course, knows what your mind is up to—and so does your body. It takes a combination of requesting, believing, and allowing—in the physical sense, if that's what it takes—in order for your desires to become reality.

CHAPTER 6

Persistence Pays Off!

We have been programmed to acknowledge that disappointment sometimes rears its ugly head. Therefore, we often tend to just accept that we *don't* always get what we wish for. But by expecting disappointment to possibly knock at the door, you are actually inviting it in. So, when you're thinking about any given possibility, whether it's a new job or a hot date, learn to say to yourself "This is going to work out for the best!" rather than "There are so many things that could go wrong!"

Now hear this! Disappointment doesn't have to come calling. Investing more time in focusing on what you want is the key—otherwise, you are fighting against yourself. That is a battle that should never be started, and it won't be, if you don't believe in giving up. In this chapter, I'll tell you how to get what you want as quickly as possible. (Hint: it's all about focus!)

What Do You Think You Want?

When you start to use the law of attraction, you may tend to get very excited. And why not? The thought of finally getting out of your rut, or becoming more healthy, or increasing your circle of social contacts, or whatever you desire is cause for excitement. You may feel like a kid in a candy store. So much to choose from! It all looks good, so how can you go wrong? You just pick what looks the best at the moment without really thinking about the other available choices.

And here's where the candy-store comparison comes to an end. Because while you're not likely to suffer any long-term problems from choosing a candy that you're not so wild about, choosing the wrong road in life can bring you a lot of heartache—so make sure to sit and consider what you want before you go asking the universe to make it happen.

And remember, unintentional thoughts take a long time to manifest. One thought is not going to do too much. It is a repeated thought that starts the ball rolling.

Be Careful What You Wish For

For years, in casual conversation, you may have said I wish ..., while wishing for this and that. Sometimes you say it wholeheartedly, while other times you merely use it as an expression and you are not really serious. For example, you might say, "I wish I'd win a million dollars tomorrow, so I can pay off all my debts and live a comfortable lifestyle."

Now typically, people don't really believe that they're going to just be handed a million dollars—not today, not tomorrow, not ever. So, what people are really saying when they use this offhand expression is "I wish I'd win a million dollars tomorrow, so I can pay off all my debts and live a comfortable lifestyle. But I know that is nearly impossible and I will have to work to get out of debt or maybe even get a second job." That is how most of us have been programmed. What we're actually doing here is not setting a positive intent of any sort—we're giving up before we've even had the chance to focus positive energy into the request!

And then there are the wishes of another sort—wishes that are so realistic you'd never spend time focusing on them, but when you repeat them over and over again, you may just get what you wish for unintentionally. Maybe you often find yourself saying, "I wish everyone would leave me alone!" Even if you aren't spending time meditating, thinking about how to get everyone to ignore you, you're still sending out a negative vibe to the universe. Don't be surprised to find yourself alone and lonely, thinking, "Oops, I didn't really mean it."

From here on, be careful about what you say aloud or to yourself as far as wishing and hoping go. You might constantly say that you wish you could get rid of your old car. Well, you might end up with no car or a car that is even worse. Make attempts to *not* wish for anything unless you are doing it with intention to bring something positive in your life.

The negative feelings that result from wishes gone awry are enough to make people believe that there are no positive outcomes for them; therefore, these folks are far less likely to use the law of attraction to turn their lives around.

Set Your Own Course Before Someone Else Does

If you don't do a little work to reach your goal, you may end up in a situation you don't desire because of failure to act. Someone else may be consciously or unconsciously focusing upon something that may affect your position or even your life. For example, if you want a job in a high-paying firm and you write your intention down and take the steps to apply for the job, but never take the time to focus your intention on securing the job, there's a good chance that someone *else* is going to be sitting in that corner office.

Even if you're called for an interview, you're very unlikely to find yourself employed by the firm if you don't go into that meeting with a positive vibration and a firm (no pun intended) belief that you are their *numero uno* candidate. Let's say you and another person are both equally qualified for the job, but the other candidate has focused, visualized, and really thought with emotion about how much she wants the job. She is more likely get hired, as she's connecting to the vibration of actually receiving the job, and you aren't. Therefore, you end up with a different job by default.

You actually helped the other person get the job by having the attitude "If it's meant to be, it's meant to be." That's a great expression, but some people use it as an excuse for not taking any action. For goodness' sake, anything and everything is (or can be) meant to be! The things that you focus your intent on are the things that *will* be—and a lack of focus means that *lack* is meant to be a major part of your life.

A General Goal Can Be Close Enough

Sometimes, people give up on asking for their desires before they even start because they feel they don't know enough about what they're asking *for*. It's always good to be specific with your requests (except when other people, like friends and lovers, are involved—more on this in Chapter 13), but general goals are often workable when you have an idea of what you want and where you want to go in life and don't know all the details.

For example, if you decide to become a nurse and want to find a job at a good hospital in the Nashville area, that may be enough to initiate your request. You don't need to know the name of the hospital where you'll work; you don't even need to know which floor you'll be on or which specific duties you'll be performing. You're not focused on a specific salary. All you want is to live and work in your career field in Nashville. That's enough for the universe to respond to, so go ahead and put those vibes out!

Specifics May Be More Your Style

Let's continue the hospital example. You are looking for a nursing position in one of three hospitals in Nashville and truly don't care which one hires you. You just want to commence with your life as a nurse.

If nothing seems to be happening, it might be time for you to think more specifically. Take the time to visit all three hospitals and see which one feels best to you. If they all seem about the same, look for something that stands out and makes you happy. It might be a fountain in their lobby, their gourmet cafeteria, or the good-looking doctor you just passed in the hall.

If they all offer something special but different, think about what's most important to you. Is having lunch in a beautiful space more important than looking at a peaceful fountain when you walk through the lobby? Are you single and hoping that someone you will meet in the workplace will be a lifelong mate? Sort through all of the possibilities and decide which scenarios fit your life (and future life) best. Once you do this, you can concentrate on asking the universe to send you work at that particular hospital.

Your Life, Your Power, Your Decisions

The fact of the matter is that our desires can take some time to come to fruition. The law of attraction does sometimes work quickly; other times, your patience is a true virtue in the process. If you get depressed or disheartened and want to jump ship on your hopes and dreams, that's up to you. I can't tell you what to do or if and when to give up on a desire. However, the question I would ask is *why* are you giving up? Are you getting discouraged because of the negative reactions of friends or family? Is it because what you asked for didn't happen fast enough for you? Or is it because deep down you are afraid of this thought becoming reality and wouldn't know what to complain about if you got what you wanted?

If you feel that you are not truly aligning with what is best for you and choose to focus on something else, then you are not giving up but moving on. If your feelings are telling you that your desire is still possible, that's when you need to consider putting more effort into it before quitting it altogether.

No one can make this decision for you. They can suggest, recommend, and even voice their thoughts, but *you* have to decide. And whatever you decide, you cannot blame others if you change your mind down the road. If your mother tells you to give up on marrying your boyfriend, for example, the ultimate responsibility for letting go of that vision of the future is yours because you are the one withdrawing your intention and energy from your request. The power and the feelings are yours and yours alone.

I Think I Can!

To be successful doesn't mean you have to suffer. Some people really are overnight successes! You can bet your bottom dollar, though, that these folks have a great belief in themselves and in attracting what they want into their lives.

Once you think you can do anything and really believe it, you are halfway home. If you start to lose confidence, look at other people who have achieved your same goals and became triumphant. Seek out success stories of those who had less than you to start out with and accomplished more than anyone (except themselves) dreamed possible.

Give heed to those who succeed. Don't read stories about those who did not succeed, even if you believe that you will not repeat their mistakes. That is still negative thought. Read about those who have persevered through rough times and come through those adversities stronger, wiser, and more successful than ever.

When you are asking the universe for the thing you want, you can go ahead and phrase part of that request as "I can …." Doing so doesn't take away from the request itself; it simply reinforces what you believe is possible. You might say, "I want to get promoted at work by the end of the year. I know I can focus my energy and make this happen."

Here are other ways to phrase "I can" statements:

"I know I can be healthy by next season."

"I know I can land this job."

"I know I can learn to accept others as they are."

"I know I can learn to let go and allow the universe to send me the things I want most."

Now these aren't the requests themselves; they're part of the process. Saying to the universe, "I know I can be a more accepting person" isn't the same as making the request "I want to be a more accepting person." The "I can" is simply a statement that presents your request to the universe in bold print, so to speak.

"I can" also implies that you have total assuredness of the situation, no matter what it is. If you said you can get your living room painted in the next 24 hours, you would probably achieve this because you know that is something you can control. You *can* have that same amount of assuredness no matter what you're asking for. And the more assuredness you have, the more likely you are to receive what you're asking for.

Visualization and Affirmations

When asking anything of the universe, you need to have positive thoughts and intentions. That means your brain has to be 100 percent on the side of your success; otherwise, your request will go out with a half-hearted and confused energy, and who knows what you'll get back?

Visualization is the process of forming mental images by using your imagination and intentionally making changes in your consciousness. An *affirmation* (also referred to as an *autosuggestion*) is a thought or phrase repeated over and over in order to create the reality of it. These techniques vary and there is no right way except for the way that works best for you.

In the law of attraction, both of these techniques for positive outcomes can be very beneficial and well worth the effort. To be sure, when one feels like giving up on a request, it often helps to sit quietly and see the positive or hoped-for outcome in the mind's eye. This can help to remind you why you wanted this thing in the first place and determine whether you choose to pursue it now.

Useful Tools or New Age Nonsense?

Sometimes when people hear the words *visualization techniques* or *affirmations* they associate them with new age thought or the new age movement. However, visualization techniques and affirmations have been around for many moons and are not exclusive to "new agers."

We hear words and phrases—affirmations—repeated in religious groups such as "Amen," and "So it is." When we visualize ourselves in our new dream home or with a new mate, those are visualizations. So you see, you've probably been using affirmations and visualizations to your benefit without even realizing it!

I suggest you employ these methods consciously and with intention. They aren't exclusive to any group and don't make you turn away from a religious faith or practice. You're simply imagining and repeating what you want in your life.

Visualizing a Positive Outcome

Visualization is really a reprogramming of the mind. (Some say it's like brainwashing yourself.) When you see what you want in life, you are focusing on it and giving it great attention. When you visualize, you are not thinking about anything else. You can do this whenever and wherever you like. The end result of positive visualization is that it puts more energy and vibration into your asking power.

Here is a visualization technique you may want to use. If this doesn't work for you, tweak it a little or find another way to visualize. (See Appendix B for some books on this subject.)

Begin by deciding what it is you want that you are going to visualize (and stick to one thing at a time). I will use a material example, but of course you can focus on more abstract desires, like good health, happiness, and the like. Pick a time when you are alone with no distractions and can put a little time into this. (A huge amount of time is not necessary if you are very strong in your vision. In fact, just a minute or two can work.) Then follow these steps:

1. Sit or lie down in a comfortable position and close your eyes.

2. Imagine yourself doing or being what you desire, and ask it of the universe. Think in the present tense: "I am ..." instead of "I will be ...." For example, if you want to weigh 125 pounds, see yourself in your bathroom or wherever you have a scale (grocery store, gym, etc.). Get as many details into the picture as you can: What are you wearing? What color is the scale? What do your surroundings look like? Now when you look at the scale, see yourself looking at the number 125.

3. Imagine now how it feels to see that number. Do you have a feeling of triumph or peacefulness, for example?

You can do this wherever and whenever, once a day or three times (or more!) a day. Tune into a quick visualization before you walk into a work meeting that's filled with doughnuts and bagels. See yourself as a lean machine before you begin your workout. And don't worry about how long you'll be committed to performing your affirmations. Just keep doing them and you will be surprised how soon your vision will come to you.

Another form of visualization is to draw what you want. (No art skill required.) If you want a new couch, for example, you might draw yourself sitting on it—make sure to get the color, style, and size just right—and you're all smiles, just lounging the afternoon away.

Warning: don't do any type of visualization techniques while driving or operating machinery. This is something to do when you are free from any distractions!

The Pros and Cons of Affirmations

Affirmations are another attempt to reprogram yourself for the better. These positively charged statements can be wonderful if they're done with intention; they can also be a waste of time if done incorrectly. In fact, when done without proper focus, they may cause you to give up too easily because you start to think you are going nowhere.

To make affirmations work for you, accept the fact that you do have the ability to change your life and that affirmations can help your growth process. If you don't believe this from the get-go, you have already sabotaged yourself. If you are at least open-minded about it, then I would recommend trying it. (It's free, you know!)

First, you have to have a thought of what it is you want, just like in visualization. Then by repetition, the thought becomes a habit, and before you know it, you believe it—and poof! You have accomplished your goal.

So, the three parts of an affirmation are ...

1. *Thought:* "I want to go back to school to become a doctor."

2. *Habit:* The above is repeated every day, several times a day, until you no longer have to remind yourself to repeat it.

3. *Belief:* "I know I'm going to be a doctor, so I'd better start studying for the MCATs."

There's no magic here; these are the fundamentals of affirmations. You have a thought of how you want the future to look, you focus on it, and before you know it, it's happening!

Affirmations are different from simply fabricating stories, because with an affirmation you truly believe that what you want can and will happen. You may have heard people say things such as, "He's lied about going to med school for so long, I think he actually believes he's going to do it!" Whether this person is a liar or a believer depends on whether he's talking about med school as a way to fortify his request or whether he's using it as a way to impress or manipulate others. As long as there's no negative intent, then nothing you say is a lie. Because if you do believe it, you will become it.

This doesn't mean that if you want to be financially stable you start spending beyond your means. But you can start visualizing or using affirmations to inspire the outcome. If you believe it to be so, the universe will correct its own mistake by saying, "Oh, he's *supposed* to be in medical school; I'd better make that happen because I am getting a direct vibration that aligns with that reality." Ta-da!

How to Do an Affirmation

There are many methods for affirmations, but let me start you with one to begin. Remember, you can tweak or change this method however you like. We are all different, so what works for one person may not work for another. Listen to your inner voice, and if something doesn't feel right, change it. You can do the following once a day or in the evening before bedtime (or both):

1. Sit or lie down in a comfortable position and close your eyes.

2. Repeat "I am relaxed" for about a minute or so, in your mind or out loud.

3. State your affirmation out loud. For example, "I am happy that I got into medical school." If you have another affirmation, you can include it, but don't do more than three different affirmations or you might lose sight of your focus. So, you can say, "I also am glad that my mother doesn't bug me about having children anymore. And I am elated that I will have enough money to pay my bills next month."

4. Repeat your affirmation(s) 5 to 10 times. You don't have to count. Just use your intuition. When you start going from meaning it to just saying words, stop.

5. Say "I am relaxed" at least three additional times.

6. Slowly get up and continue your day or evening. Or if you're lying in bed, just go to sleep.

After a while, these affirmations will become a habit, like brushing your teeth, so try to do them at the same time each day. But if you are a person who likes spontaneity, that can work, too. Just get to know yourself and what works best for you.

Now remember: these affirmations are the things that you are requesting of the universe. They haven't come to fruition yet. By repeating them out loud, you're focusing a great amount of energy into them and eventually, the affirmations will become your reality. *Eventually* can mean only a day away. Don't limit yourself to thinking all good things take time. If your emotion is backing up your visualizations or affirmations, you may be pleasantly surprised.

Release Yourself from Yourself

Have you ever done something wrong or something that you were sorry for? You may have said things like "Nobody can make me feel any worse than I already feel." Most of us have been there. And it's good to let others know that you are aware of what you did, and that they don't need to point it out. The issue should stop there. Let it go, and think about not making those types of errors in the future. Better yet, don't think about it at all.

It's time to stop blaming others, circumstances, and yourself for anything that's lacking in your life. By virtue of the fact that you are investigating this book, perhaps you are searching for ways to improve and grow, so let's get on with it! Then again, you might be reading this book because it was the only thing around, or a loved one gave it to you and you feel obligated, or you feel it's such nonsense that you want to see what it is all about so you can confirm your feelings were right. Hmm … I rather think that no matter what your feelings are, you've attracted this information into your life. And now that it's here, you can choose to use it for the better or go back to the old methods that weren't working so well.

Stop being your own worst enemy, and learn how to better yourself and your life!

Talking Yourself into—or Out of—Your Goals

If at first you don't succeed … don't decide to change your goals so quickly. You wanted to be a firefighter but flunked the exam, so now you decide to be a computer technician. No, no, no.

It's one thing to recognize that a career move or a goal might not be what you are aligning with energetically. (In other words, the job you wanted so badly is draining the life out of you.) But to give up after the first defeat (or should I say, lack of vision) is perhaps a bit lazy, no? For those of you who are saying, "No, it isn't; I've had it and I'm going to do something else!" you need to take time to really think about your present situation and not act on emotion. Take that hostile or negative feeling and turn it into passion for something you want. Just remember, there's a fine line between passion and anger. Let's go with positive, creative passion and leave the anger at the door.

Be Happy While Waiting for Happiness

Once you have decided to give everything you have to your intention, the next step is easy: be happy.

There are those of you who might say that it's easy for *me* to suggest that—*you're* the one with ill health, no way to pay the bills, a partner who is a jerk, a family who won't lend a hand, and a job you hate or no job at all, and so forth. But there you go again, focusing on what you don't want in life! There must be something out there that makes you happy. Is it the sunrise or the full moon? How about a rainstorm with a lightning show that's better than anything you can pay for? The sound of the wind or the songs of falling waters?

But back to making a living and paying your credit card bills, right? The point is no matter what's going on in your life, you can find a good thing or two to be grateful for. And that simple act of gratitude can help to sustain you enough to focus your energy on the things you want to improve your life (instead of focusing on where you are at the moment). You might have credit card bills, but you also have the eyes to read the bills, hands to open the bills, and people in your life who create the bills (your family). Tap into the positive energy of the good things in your life and then you can make a request with a positive intention and plan for the future.

CHAPTER 7

Compassion Is the Fashion

The author Ruth Smeltzer said, "You have not lived a perfect day, even though you have earned your money, unless you have done something for someone who cannot repay you." These are strong words that relate perfectly to how compassion plays into the law of attraction.

The law of attraction is usually thought of as a way to get what you want in life: wealth, career, popularity, and so on. To some this may seem very shallow and materialistic. But there is nothing wrong with wanting or having those things. I believe we are on this planet to experience happiness and love as well as to have a better understanding of what the universe has to offer. If that translates into a wealthy life filled with fast cars and lots of dates, so be it.

It's when we try to achieve those things from a selfish standpoint that things can go haywire. It's fine, for example, to want wealth, but it's not alright to look down on those who aren't as fortunate. It's also not alright to say, "Well, they created their own problems; too bad for them." You know what you're doing in these scenarios? You're creating a negative vibe that will come back to bite you. Helping others without pity or an expectation of reimbursement (of any sort—emotional, physical, or financial) is what compassion is all about. And compassion is part and parcel of the law of attraction.

Not Such a Secret

Compassion is often defined as having sympathy for others. We're not going with that definition here. The heart of compassion, as it relates to the law of attraction, is helping others without expecting recognition or a reward of any sort. Pity isn't part of this party. Pity only makes negative vibrations stronger and keeps a person down.

Often we forget that we are all part of each other, and hence we can become selfish and detached from other's dilemmas. But because we are all energy and we work at a vibrational level, we can't disconnect ourselves from each other's dilemmas. By having compassion for one another, the positive vibrational energy of the planet increases—and that's good for all of us.

Love Your Neighbor

Whether we're rich or poor, we are all interrelated. The people who we refer to as rich, at least in a materialistic way, may have inherited fortunes; others won their wealth, and then there are those who worked hard for it. Are any of the above better than the other? Not really, as they all attracted it to themselves, usually without even knowing it. Those who want to be successful *believe* they can be. They attract what they desire because they expect it.

Even inherited money has been attracted by those who accumulated the riches in the first place. As the money is passed from generation to generation, a vibrational level of wealth keeps flowing. There's an expectation that the money will continue to come in … and it does!

Because wealth can be a precarious situation (due to where your focus is and what you're attracting), the rich should have compassion for those who are struggling financially. Wealthy people are just better at attracting money. As I said, sometimes they do it by default and don't even know they're using the law of attraction.

"Uh-huh," I hear you saying, "but what about people who lose their fortunes?" All this means is that they attracted wealth but then did not keep that positive attraction going. So, once you receive what you're asking for, remember to *maintain* a positive attitude!

A poor person can often make matters worse by thinking she is destined to always be poor. In fact, I've seen down-and-out friends refuse to think positive thoughts because they don't want to be disappointed if they don't get their desired results.

How can those of us who are better off help those with money problems or any other problems, for that matter? The best way to help is to set an example by showing others that a positive attitude creates a vibe that comes back to you. Go ahead and lend a hand, but make sure you're teaching a struggling friend how to help herself. It's like that old expression "Give a man a fish and he will eat for a day. Teach him to fish and he will eat for the rest of his life."

Words like "you poor thing" and "I feel so sorry for you" aren't really compassionate because they only help to perpetuate the negative feelings of helplessness. Instead, send some positive energy to a down-in-the-dumps friend by saying, "I know everything is going to work out for you."

Is There Any Way Out?

Sometimes people have major problems in their lives that create such a negative situation, it seems they almost can't get out of it. The negativity mounts and the bad vibrations compound. Therefore, it's a waste of time to tell someone who has the weight of the world on his shoulders, so to speak, to be happy. He's stuck in a hole, and he doesn't see a way out.

It's one thing to help in a financial way, but what about when a friend is struggling with health or depression issues? What's the most compassionate way to deal with her? Try to distract your friend and turn her negative thoughts toward the positive, no matter how briefly. Take her to a movie, dinner, or talk about something that does not involve her present concern. In other words, don't feed a bad situation by dwelling on it. Only *positive* energy can bring about positive change.

Cruel to Be Kind

We can use the law of attraction to show compassion for others, but we should do it in a way other than pity. People do not need to know how sorry you feel for them. It only confirms their belief that everyone knows how pathetic they are.

If friends or family are always complaining, point it out to them. Mention that they should think of the good things and not the bad. Every time I see a friend who starts complaining, I will stop and say, "So, tell me something good that happened today." If he says he can't think of anything, tell him the mere fact that he *can* think is good. Maybe this doesn't sound like the most nurturing way to go about changing a mind-set, but it's a method for pointing the person in the direction of positive energy. That's the most compassionate thing I can think of.

In short, refuse to feed into another person's negativity. It is not sympathetic or compassionate to do so; it only makes matters worse. In Chapter 18, I'll talk more about how to help others.

Empathy and Love Complete Your Intent

The law of attraction teaches us that we create our own lives, whether good or not so good. Some people can carry this too far and become egotistical when they learn how to use the law of attraction.

I have heard people—those who have supposedly mastered the art of using the law of attraction—say things such as "I can't help her; she wants the impossible." While this may seem true, it's important to remember that most everything is possible if we invest our belief in the power of the universe. Furthermore, we need to have compassion for people who are *trying* to move in a more positive direction. Not only are they working on their own happiness, they'll be spreading joy to others in the process. And just remember: the more compassionate we are toward others, the more compassion will be given to us.

Show Some Compassion for Yourself

Having compassion and understanding for others is a huge component of the law of attraction. Think of it this way: if you judge others harshly or simply choose not to care about them one way or the other, you increase your negative-vibe rating. When you take the time to care about other people, you start to feel something that sends your positive vibrations shooting through the roof. (Is that love, you wonder?) You can't help but feel good when you invest your positive energy in other people.

There's one more person who deserves a break on the universal level: you! It's self-defeating to love others but harbor doubts about what lies ahead for you. Let's say, for example, that you and your sister are both divorced and looking for the next great love in your lives. You have no problem supporting your sis by saying, "You are an amazing person. Any man would be lucky to have you; he's out there somewhere. Don't you realize all the great surprises that life has in store for you?" Meanwhile, you stand before the mirror cursing the gray hairs sprouting from your temples and the extra 10 pounds you've gained sitting home alone every night with a carton of ice cream. Do you realize what you're doing in this situation? You're telling the universe that you believe in its power for other people, but not for yourself! That's quite a condescending attitude—not to mention, you're not getting what you want!

Take the time each day to remind yourself that the universe delivers to those who ask and believe. But the first thing that you have to believe is that you are as deserving of the things you want as other people are. I don't care what you've done in the past, or what your fears are regarding the future. Take one day and forget everything but the here and now and answer this question: what is it that I want? If all it takes to receive this thing is for you to be kinder to yourself and believe it can happen, are you willing to do that?

Methods for Including Compassion in Requests

When asking for things in your life, you can embrace the idea of compassion or even forgiveness.

There are no rules as to what you can ask for or what you can attract to yourself. The important thing still remains that you do not dwell on what you don't have or what state of mind you aren't in. You want to focus on what you do want and what state of mind you want to be in.

But don't fear every thought you have! Most of us have sad thoughts now and again. It can take a long time to turn your negative state of mind around. By simply becoming aware of this concept and working on it a little bit each day, you'll find peace of mind in due time—as long as you believe you can.

By thinking you don't want to be depressed forever, you can depress yourself even more. How? You're focusing on the depression instead of using your emotion, intention, and compassion for yourself to focus on how great life will be when you feel happy again.

As for focusing on being a more compassionate person, you can absolutely do that—just be careful with your language. Don't think "I'm sorry I can't do more for my friend"; instead think "I want to help my friend more." The former statement is concentrating on what you aren't doing and attracting more of a helpless feeling into your life!

Lack Attracts Lack

Compassion and love can be a springboard to assist us in bringing what we want to us faster, as these are emotions. In Chapter 5, I talked about how thoughts backed up with passion and emotion are heard most clearly by the universe, so compassion and love can only better any given situation.

If you are looking for compassion from others, what you are really doing is looking for others to help you or feel sorry for you. There is nothing wrong with wanting people to assist you in finding a job, for example, if they have the ability to do so. But if you complain to people or intentionally try to make them feel sorry for you, your focal point is on what you are lacking, and as you know by now, that's not going to fly with the universe. You'll only attract more negativity into your life.

So, how do you ask for help for yourself while including compassion in that request? You might think to yourself, "I want Glenn to help me financially. Then I can get on my feet and pay him back when I secure a job." You *don't* want to say, "I want Glenn to feel so sorry for me that he offers to loan me money. He knows I am always broke, and nobody gives me a chance. Plus, he's loaded and he can afford to help me. But if I ever get a job I would pay him back."

Take a minute to see the differences between the two requests. In the second situation, Glenn isn't going to loan you the money out of love and compassion, but out of pity and possibly a feeling of obligation.

In the first situation, however, the request comes from a completely different emotional place. You want to better your situation, and you're looking to someone who can help you do that. Glenn doesn't see you standing there with your hand out; he sees you planning a bright new future, and he's hoping it works out. That's compassion in action.

Your Turn!

When you help someone else, center your thoughts on the fact that this action will make a difference and help put the person in a better space. Do not take the attitude, "I'll help him once, and let someone else help him next time." By thinking that way, you are not truly showing love and compassion. You are actually making things worse because the vibration you are sending out is that your friend will have to borrow money again in the future. In essence, you are physically giving with one hand, but vibrationally taking away with the other.

I want to caution you, however, about taking on too much and knowing when to back away for the time being. I have a former friend—we'll call her Ashley. She was a very negative soul, convinced that her life was lousy beyond belief and it could not improve. No matter what kind of compassion or distraction friends offered to her, including advice for focusing on the positive things in her life (because there were several very good things happening to her!), she couldn't shift her vibration toward gratitude, acceptance, or anything on the positive spectrum.

After trying to help her for about a year, I had to back away because I felt my vibration being pulled into her negative orbit. If things had continued as they were going, I might have pulled another person into negativity, and that's the opposite of what anyone wants or needs. I had to have compassion for myself in this situation and say, "I have done what I can for now. If Ashley is open to discussion in the future, I will try to help her at that time."

Working Compassion into Your Life

There are other ways to use compassion in your life. There are those whose greatest happiness comes from giving. Let's say you love to help people and have decided to go into a medical or healing field but need the funds to help pay for your education.

When you are in the asking or desire mode and looking for the financing to come into your life, you can use that compassion within you for a fast "lift off." Feel the bliss you would feel helping others. Think about how you would change lives for the better. Don't think about how ill your patients will be and how you would hate to see them die in your presence.

Go with the positive and the idea that you will be the one to put them in a situation of wellness, which will be gratifying. In this way, you are using your compassionate attitude to help you initially, and that, in turn, will enable you to eventually help others. It's a win-win situation.

The law of attraction enlightens us to the philosophy that we all have the ability to help ourselves, and that pity gets us nowhere fast. Accept help from others and feel the gratitude for their help; likewise, help others from a place of love. The positive energy you create with compassion will astound you!

PART 3

What Goes Around Comes Around

This is the fun part! Once you've learned how the law of attraction works, it's time to put it to use. In the following chapters, I give you methods for asking, believing, and receiving the things that you want. I also talk about children and the law of attraction, as well as how to know if your request is greedy.

CHAPTER 8

Universal Appeals

When we set our focus and intention, who is it we are really appealing to or asking? Is it God, the universe, or an alien being? We keep talking about the universe, so let's define who and what we're talking to when we talk about asking. For some of you, it may not be essential to know, but others may be wondering about specifics at this point.

Some people need to have a solid idea of who or what they are asking things of to make it easier for them to stay positive. Just remember that there is no one right or wrong word or vision to describe this source.

First Things First

As you continue to use the law of attraction, it is important to bear something in mind: you are adding a new process that you probably have not consciously participated in before. It may seem impossible to reroute your way of thinking and start all over from scratch, but you must get rid of some of your old methods to make way for a bright new future.

I'm not picking on or judging anyone. We're all programmed from the time we're children to believe and to not believe in certain things, rules, concepts—you name it. Good thing for us that as adults we have the power to reevaluate those ideas and decide whether we want to put our energy into them now, or whether we want to open our minds to new possibilities.

Say So Long to Your Old Methods

Here's one piece of common sense advice I have for you: stop using the methods that haven't worked for you in the past. That's like watching a bird who repeatedly insists on flying into a glass door! He's not going to get through, no matter how hard he throws himself against it, and he may very well end up hurting himself in the process.

If you continue to use these old methods, that's also not investing your belief in the law of attraction. It's like saying, "Well, I hear this law of attraction thing works for some people, but I don't really believe in that kind of thing. It's better for me to keep repeating the same mistakes I've been making rather than trying something new, anyway."

If your old method was simply having a positive attitude, then keep that—but add passion and real hope that things in life will go your way. *That's* using the law of attraction!

Every Positive Thought Gets You Closer

If you always see the glass as half drained, you need to get on the glass-is-half-full, positive-attitude train.

In other words, you can't walk around saying, "Oh, sure, everything is going to work out just the way I want it," when inside your head, you're hearing, "Suuuuuuuure it will." Throw that negativity out, and replace it with genuine positive belief.

And it doesn't help your case to walk around pretending you're happy or pretending to believe in the power of the law of attraction. The only person you may fool is yourself if your positive perspective isn't sincere. You might be better off not commenting on things at all than to say something you feel isn't honest. One of the fundamentals of this law is that you believe in it wholeheartedly—or at least keep an open mind. Saying empty words does not a happy reality make.

For those of you who are reading this and thinking, "Sure, it's easy for her to say, but she doesn't have the life or the troubles I do," I understand. I am not suggesting you stick your head in the sand like an ostrich and pretend you don't have problems. But especially when you're dealing with something you have very little control over (a wayward adult child who's landed in jail, for example, or a hurricane barreling toward your home), I do recommend that you try to think of something that makes you happy or something that you *want* to happen in the future. (Picture the day that wayward son is paroled or the storm blowing back out to sea.)

Know that you are on the edge of transforming your life because you want to be healthy, happy, and successful. Those are the thoughts that will keep you from slipping back into negativity as usual.

There's a great quote from artist Francesca Reigler: "Happiness is an attitude. We either make ourselves miserable, or happy and strong. The amount of work is the same." Truer words were never spoken!

Neutral over Negative

This next story will hopefully illustrate my point that you can turn your negative thoughts into thoughts that are, at the very least, neutral.

Gail worked at a post office in San Francisco, California. She loved her job except for the fact that she had to work with Joyce, a seasoned employee who thought because she was retiring in a year, she didn't need to work as hard as everyone else and also developed a difficult attitude. She was older, wiser (in her own opinion), had been there longer, so she could call the shots.

Joyce took the attitude that she was doing the customers a personal favor by helping them; she never smiled and was never pleasant. The bottom line was that she resented having to work at her age, and this was reflected in her disposition toward her customers.

Gail tried very hard to be nice to Joyce, but Joyce had a mind-set that she would not even be pleasant on Fridays on principle. Gail hated working with her and at the end of the day would think about the horrible way Joyce treated customers and even her superiors. Her bosses almost looked as though they were afraid of her and never confronted her about anything.

One day, Gail had forgotten to do something to wrap up the business day, and Joyce verbally attacked her. Gail apologized and corrected her error, but later that night, she thought about how Joyce overreacted, and she knew that the following day at the monthly meeting, Joyce would most likely express that Gail had made a mistake. She was obsessing all night about Joyce. She wanted Joyce to get stung by a swarm of bees and not go to work. She wanted Joyce's car to run out of gas, or a truck to dump a load of manure all over Joyce while she stood on the corner by Starbucks.

Then it dawned on Gail—like a falling star she didn't expect to see—she needed to be positive and not negative. So, instead of thinking about all of the horrible things that she wanted to happen to Joyce, she thought the opposite. She pictured Joyce happy and retiring early.

Gail went from feeling pure hatred and thinking of negative ways to get rid of Joyce to wishing positive things would happen so Joyce would leave early.

The next day, at the meeting, Joyce was the same old ornery person she normally was, but Gail was different. She became *in*different. She took the attitude that she would not let Joyce transform her one way or the other. So, Gail was the winner, as she did not enable this situation to affect her attitude about work, her relationships with others, or her outlook in general. Sometimes, we let people get hold of our emotions and run wild with them. Now you have the answer: neutralize them!

Ask and You Shall Receive

We've talked about asking with passion and emotion. We've also discussed what to call the higher power that you request things of; you can call it God, the universe, or whomever or whatever you choose, but if none of these are a particularly good fit for you, then they won't work. It's that simple. But fortunately, you're not limited to envisioning only one or two higher powers.

Envisioning a Symbol

When you do your asking, it may help to visualize something concrete, instead of an abstract idea like the universe. Some people have a real issue with this, thinking that they have to get into some kind of heathen belief system (worshipping false gods, etc.). This, in turn, leads to the mistaken belief that the law of attraction is all about witchcraft, the dark arts, and heaven knows what else.

Not true. The law of attraction isn't some trick that fringe groups are playing on you, trying to convert you to another religion or belief. The law of attraction works for people of every belief system. Focusing on something to achieve your goal isn't meant to be a form of worship; it's simply a way to quiet the mind, connect with your inner energy, and send it out in the form of a request.

This thing you focus on doesn't have to be human or even anything mystical. It can be as simple as ...

- A circle that surrounds you.
- A box filled with your intent and request.
- A lemniscate (or the infinity symbol) revolving.

The symbol may be moving or stationary. Visualizing things like the sun, sky, stars, or ocean can also be considered. To focus on your intention, you can picture the waves rolling from far out in the ocean to the shore of the beach, or imagine lying on the ground and counting the stars. Anything that helps to eliminate distractions around you and relax you is a positive symbol.

The point of using the law of attraction is to enable yourself to zone out and tap into your mind's energy. If you can do this best by imagining a tree, a stream, or a bird, then go ahead and use it. After all, these are all part of the universe (if that's what you believe in); so essentially, they're all part of the bigger picture.

Tuning in to Your God

Now, having just said that, you are under no obligation to participate in worshipping anything or anyone in order to get the law of attraction to work for you; you can if you want to. Use your God as your focal point for relaxation and concentration. Picture him or her however you like. If white robes and a long beard is how you see God, do that. Some of you may want to picture Jesus, others may want to picture Buddha, and others may think Confucius is the ticket to exercising their energy efficiently. There is no right or wrong person, symbol, or way to do this. It's whatever works for you.

In addition, you may want to visualize saints, angels, and so forth. You are doing the asking, so make yourself comfortable with whomever you see as a higher power and request their guidance and assistance.

Your Inner Self

You may not relate to symbols, religious images, or spiritual pictures. You may not believe in a source outside of yourself, but rather, you believe that the power that makes things happens comes from yourself. If that is the case, then think of your inner self or being.

Your inner self or as some might call it, your *spirit*, is a strong source of intuition and strength, whether you realize it and use it regularly or not. Do you know those times in life when everything is going wrong and yet you keep trudging through somehow? That's your inner self carrying you on its back, so to speak. Everyone has this essence, and everyone can learn to harness its power.

When you make a request, you can use your inner self to fuel your energy and send it out to whichever force you believe is at work. Think of this as flipping a switch and illuminating your own power source to work within you and produce outward results.

Create Your Own Method

So, let's say that none of these ideas are working for you. If you want to use the law of attraction but need a different way to focus on something, individualize it. I keep saying that there's no right or wrong way to do this—but in truth, there *is* a wrong way to ask something of the universe, God, Buddha, nature, or what have you: if you can't connect your energy to that of the higher power when you make your request, then you can forget about seeing the kinds of results you're hoping for. That's like talking with someone over a static-filled phone connection. Not everything is going to go through as clearly as you'd hoped.

I interviewed a small group about this very topic and they shared a few interesting ways that helped them focus during the asking process:

- Lighting a candle
- Listening to Music
- Petting a dog or cat
- Swimming
- Contemplating nature

Basically, these methods help people to move into an altered state of consciousness, almost like meditation. Being calm and relaxed when asking for what you want is of the utmost importance, but you don't need to make this into a long, drawn-out process. So, while meditation can be helpful, it's not at all necessary. All thoughts that focus on what you want will help the process.

What Are the Rules?

Unfortunately we live in a world where there are rules and more rules, so we expect there to be rules surrounding all things, even the law of attraction. For lack of a better way to put it, there are rules, but they aren't the same rules you'd abide by in a class of some kind or even in your own home. I prefer to call the law-of-attraction rules a *system* or a *method*.

Understanding the law of attraction is the biggest rule. You create that which you focus upon, whether positive or negative. If you don't deliberately ask for that which you want, you will bring forth things in your life by default, good or bad. Here, in a nutshell, are the three "biggies":

- You must know what you want.
- You must ask with emotion and feeling.
- You must allow yourself to receive the things you asked for.

Those are the basic rules that are reiterated throughout the book. I'll add to them a bit in this next section.

No Limits, but You Must Prioritize

I've told you several times in this book that there are no limits to asking. You can ask for 1 thing, or you can ask for 10 things. You can focus on using the law of attraction in a one-time-only situation, or you can use it over and over again for big and small issues.

The only thing I would warn against is asking for too many things at one time—not because it's not possible to receive it all, but because by requesting everything all at once, you are not focusing on one particular desire. Hence, your vibration may not be strong. If you put your efforts into one desire or, at most, a few at a time, you will have a better chance of the vibration being stronger and seeing great results.

For example, if you want a new car, a new house, a new job, and a new romance, think of what is most important.

If a new job is on the top of your list, start by asking for it by using the methods throughout this book to make it so. You should be able to feel if you have done the asking correctly because it should make you feel good when you think about it later.

Once you feel you have done your best to start the cosmic ball rolling, don't forget about it, but know it is coming your way; then move on to the next item, and so forth.

Getting Rid of Mental Clutter

Some people—particularly highly educated folks—have a real aversion to meditation or visualization. They feel that their brains are highly trained and there's no reason to take time out of the day to focus on a simple request. Well, I'm here to tell you that when your brain is filled with many desires and you want everything now, you may need to do a little mental cleaning and organizing before you make a request of the universe. Otherwise, you will end up with more clutter and nothing that works. So, it went in the story of George.

George started investigating the law of attraction and was very excited about the possibility of getting what he felt he deserved in life. This excitement was perfect for him to attract what he wanted. However, he didn't take the time to prepare his mind before focusing his energy on his requests. His first set of requests was a real doozy. First, he wanted to be able to pay off all his credit cards. Then he decided he wanted not only to pay off credit cards, but also have enough money in the bank to retire early. Then he wanted a new, paid-for BMW. And because he wanted to be realistic (and not demanding), he thought he would grant the universe 7 days to produce! And if he didn't get those things in 7 days, he was done with the law of attraction.

Seven days came and went, and no money for credit cards, no money to retire early, and not even a windshield blade for the new BMW materialized.

So, why didn't George get what he wanted? Was he too greedy? No. I told you earlier that the universe has no problem with giving you exactly what you want. The universe *does* have an issue with negative attitudes, however. George's requests weren't coming from a place of pure belief. He was challenging the universe by essentially saying, "If you can't deliver everything I want in 1 week— and I'm not at all sure that you can—then you and I are through." Imagine saying something similar to your boss (who, like the universe, has a large measure of control over your environment and has no need to impress you). What do you think would happen?

George could have improved his chances of succeeding by doing two things: first, he should have spent some time focusing on his belief in the law of attraction. In earlier chapters, I told you that sometimes it's best to ask for small things first (like a great parking spot) because it's easier for you to believe that the universe can send those things your way. Once your belief in the law of attraction is unwavering, you truly *know* that the universe can deliver on your bigger requests.

Second, George's requests were all over the place, which is fine if you have a firmly rooted belief in the universe, but is another common point of difficulty for beginners. You have to develop the ability to focus your positive energy on your requests, which can be tricky (though not impossible) if you're asking for several things at once. This is a definite skill that often involves meditation, visualization, and/or affirmations—in other words, clearing the mind and seeing your intended result—and George didn't want to be bothered with all of that preparation. He started the race without running shoes. In fact, there wasn't even a track.

Never Too Late to Ask Again

If you go to a restaurant, do you keep asking the waiter for the same entrée until he brings it to the table? I hope not! You order once and then wait for your meal to arrive, knowing that it is being prepared for you. This is similar to the asking process in the law of attraction.

Asking over and over again is different from visualizing what you want. Therefore, you should intentionally ask for what you want *once* with great passion and then, rather than making repetitive requests, use repetitive focusing without going through the whole process of focusing on an object and making the "I want" statement. Simply sit down, close your eyes, and see yourself in that new job. Feel the excitement of having the job and looking at your first paycheck.

If you do find yourself asking for the same thing over and over again, and each time your intention and vibration are the same, it shouldn't do you any harm. But typically, we don't have the same feelings about something every day, or we are not in the same mood, and I believe that asking without the proper focus can hurt your case more than help it.

If you have quit your asking process (see Chapter 6 for details about moving on), then you can always begin the entire thing again, using the same great passion and excitement the second time around.

Give It Time ... but How Much Time?

According to the law of attraction, we should be able to get what we want immediately. But because we have already created situations in our life before we knew about the law of attraction, a lot of damaging, unhelpful thoughts and situations have to be negated by our new, more positive thoughts. The negative vibrations don't go away completely, but they are less powerful when we take our focus off them. Once the new thoughts outweigh the vibration of our former thoughts, things will happen faster, but not necessarily within the hour.

Any book about positive thinking or any good motivational speaker will suggest you give attention to a solution for a problem and not the problem itself. The case is the same here. Don't think about why it's taking so long to get what you want. Do something to propel you toward your desire a little faster.

Your first focused request will most likely not occur right away. It takes a build-up of positive thoughts backed by inner knowing that you are aligning with what you want. If time is a concern of yours (most of us want everything yesterday), add that into your initial asking: "I want to have a new job by February of this year," for example. The trick here is to believe it's *possible* for that to occur within that time frame. If you say "I want my boss to give me a raise tomorrow" and you know you are not due for a raise and haven't done anything special to warrant one anyway, you are stopping your own progress because in your mind, you *know* that it's very unlikely to happen. On the other hand, if you meditate and focus on getting a raise and/or a new position and you truly believe that it's a realistic request, then you're playing with a different hand, so to speak.

Going back to the restaurant example, when you place your order, you have no doubt that the waiter will bring your food within a reasonable amount of time. It may come slower than what you've experienced in the past, but you know one way or the other you will receive it before you faint from hunger. You have gone through this before, and you understand how the process works. Once you see for yourself how successful the law of attraction can be, you will believe it more. And with that proof and a stronger belief, things will come to you faster.

One last point I want to include: sometimes, our negativity is coming from an actual mood disorder. If you find yourself in a severe depression, don't be ashamed to get professional help. Once you are in a better frame of mind, you can start using the law of attraction—with great success!

CHAPTER 9

Evaluating Requests

Some people look at the law of attraction and think to themselves, "Interesting concept, but with all this talk about material things, better jobs, and vacations, isn't this a tad bit greedy?"

I couldn't disagree more. We haven't been put on this planet to suffer or even to test our mettle (in other words, to see how much unhappiness we can handle). I believe we're here to learn about our true nature, and part of that is going with the flow of the universe. Moving with that flow (as opposed to fighting it) ensures contentment, at the very least.

Determining the direction the universe wants you to move in is a big project, and that's part of what the law of attraction is all about. Some people are called to help others; some people aren't. The helpers tend to be most concerned about asking for things for themselves. In this chapter, I'll explain why *want* isn't your typical four-letter word.

Need vs. Greed

Some religious traditions (and heck, plenty of nonreligious theories) teach us that the key to happiness is giving to others. There's certainly nothing wrong with that; as we talked about in Chapter 7, a world without compassion would be a mighty scary place. Having compassion for yourself is crucial, especially when it comes to protecting yourself from greed, which as you'll read in this section, isn't just a harmless emotion. It's something that can mess with your asking and receiving processes big time.

Want + Envy = Greed

Wanting things is not greed. You are supposed to be happy in this lifetime, and there is enough of everything to go around for everyone. If no one ever wanted anything, we'd still be living in caves.

Want becomes greed when it intertwines with envy. When you focus on what you don't have (while looking around at what others do have and wishing it were yours), you create a negative energy. Remember: the law of attraction works by stating and focusing on the things that you want. If you sit around thinking, "I hate this house. It's so small and in bad shape. Why can't we have a nice place like my sister and her family?" then your energy is creating a negative swirl in the universe. This isn't helping you to better your situation; it's keeping you right where you are, aching for more.

Try this: when greed creeps into your thoughts, simply stop and refocus. Don't think about your sister's home; see yourself in your new home. Feel the relief of having more space, of not having holes in the wall, of having central air conditioning … whatever you want!

Who Says Wanting Is Bad?

Worrying that you are now or will become greedy by requesting things for yourself is a negative thought. And you know by now that negative thoughts work against your true nature, your energy, and your focus. Negative thoughts keep you stuck in the same place, so kick those worries about greed to the curb and *allow* yourself to want!

I understand this concern about greed, though, especially among helpers. Asking for something for yourself may cause you to think that you are taking away from others who have less, or it may remind you that others would be grateful for the things you have. You may think that you should be happy and settle for what you have, and that you don't really need anything more. But who defines *need*?

Sure, we can focus on the basic needs for survival: food, shelter, and clothing. But what about the need to feel connected to other people, or the need to feel as though your work is meaningful, or the need to feel as though you've left your mark on this world? I personally don't think that these are any less important to human survival than food and water.

If you need to be surrounded by beauty to feel as though you're doing well in life, then so be it. Set your intent and ask for it. If you need to find a soul mate to feel as though your life is complete, there's nothing wrong with that. We aren't all cut from the same cloth; every single human being needs different things to feel simultaneously energized and at peace. So, lose your worries about greed and work with *your* nature. When you're happy, you can make others happy. And that's anything *but* greedy.

Don't Be Needy!

Now that I've talked all about need, I'm going to go back and reverse myself—but just a little. When you ask the universe for the things you need in your life, don't phrase them as *needs*—phrase them as *wants*. *Need* implies that you're lacking something essential for everyday life. As you know by now, lack attracts lack. *Want*, on the other hand, implies that you could take this thing or leave it ... but you'd really much rather take it.

The emotion you emanate with need is negative. It implies that if you don't receive what you're asking for (or if this thing were to disappear after you've received it), you'd be in a state of deprivation. Don't worry about the word *need* slipping into everyday conversation; it's inevitable. But when you get down to business and attach emotion to your request, substitute *want* for *need* and watch what happens!

For example, when you say, "I need a boyfriend!" that implies that you somehow aren't complete without a man in your life. But when you say, "I want a boyfriend," the implication is that you could take a man or leave him (but that you'd rather take him). It's a matter of semantics, I know, but there's a definite difference in the vibrational energy of the two words.

Is This Helping?

Years ago, I was talking to a friend of mine, telling her I tend to put other people before myself. She said, "Sometimes when you do what is best for yourself, it ends up being what is best for other people." I never thought of that, and frankly, I struggled to believe it, until I tried it one day.

I had made a date to go shopping with a friend of mine. The day arrived for the big event and I just didn't feel like going. I had no special reason, but I just was not in the shopping mood. I didn't want to disappoint my friend, so I was going to force myself to go.

Then I decided to try out this philosophy. I called my friend and said I wasn't in the mood to go, and asked if we could make plans for some other time. She replied that she wasn't in the mood to go either but didn't want to hurt my feelings, so she was going to force herself to go for my sake.

Now can you imagine the scene if we had both gone for the other's sake? We would have been two unhappy women at the mall, forcing niceties and enthusiasm because we thought it would make the other one happy. In other words, it would have been a waste of time, energy, and a day. We would not have been helping one another at all; we would have been draining each other's positive vibes!

Go Ahead—Look Out for Number One!

I'm saying exactly what you think I'm saying: it's okay to put yourself first sometimes, and it's alright to ask for things for yourself. But you may still be wondering how a seemingly selfish request will help others. For some people, this is a major issue and they can't take a step forward in the asking process without knowing how their actions will affect others.

Well, here's where you have to focus on the best possible outcomes and eliminate thoughts of greed. Let's say that you want a new car, and you set your intention and focus and request this of the universe. Maybe you feel it's unrealistic to expect a new car to just appear in your driveway. But have some faith! The point is that you ask for a new car and the universe provides the means for you to get one. It's not up to us to worry about how it's going to happen. Just allow it to happen, and know that it will happen.

So, how might having a dependable set of wheels help the people in your life?

- If you have children, you'll undoubtedly be driving them to fun activities.
- You'll be able to do errands for friends and neighbors.
- You may want to use the car to participate in charitable work, like Meals on Wheels.

I know, these sound like small things, but they're very real and make a big difference in the lives of people who aren't able to drive. Consider the alternatives (kids unable to get to basketball practice, friends and neighbors unable to get to doctors' appointments, charities needing a good person to help them out), and you'll see that your request for an automobile really isn't so selfish after all.

Here's another example, one that has a little less selflessness attached to it. You think, "Boy, it would be great to win the lottery. I'd love to have all of that money. Plus, I'd help everyone I know." This request is obviously first and foremost self-serving (again, nothing wrong with that), but it does contain a sincere desire to help others, which is admirable.

Two things: I'm not going to tell you to get rid of requests that are essentially just for the heck of it—that's the fun part of life! But be careful how you phrase this kind of request. Focus on the want, not on what you and your friends are lacking. (Don't think, "I need to win this money because I'm just so darn broke." Put a positive spin on it, or the universe will hear "need … broke …" and send you those things in a not-so-neat package!)

Consider the Outcome

These are relatively harmless examples, so when it comes to requests that can have a bigger impact on your life and the lives of others, you have to look deeper within yourself and figure out whether you're helping or hurting yourself in the long run. For example, if you ask for a job where you don't have to do a single thing all day long, will that be a good thing for you—will you find ways to keep busy?—or the worst thing that ever happened—will it kill your energy and make you feel useless? If you request that a shelter down the street from you close its doors because you don't like seeing homeless people hanging around, what effect will that have on others? If you want to see your boss brought down in a scandal so that you can have his job, what might the fallout from that be? Might the company close altogether, causing 100 people to lose their jobs?

I'm not judging these requests—sometimes they may well be the best thing for everyone. (Maybe the company actually expands dramatically with you in the CEO chair!) I just want you to have a clear, full picture of what could happen when your request comes to fruition. You don't want to help create a situation that's worse than the situation you're in right now!

The Law of Attraction and Prayer

Victor Hugo, famed author of *Les Misérables*, said, "Certain thoughts are prayers. There are moments when, whatever be the attitude of the body, the soul is on its knees."

We have prayers where we ask for what we want. There are prayers where we give thanks for what we have. And there are prayers where we focus on what we need—and those prayers are backed by much negative emotion. (How many people fall to their knees crying for help because of something they lack in their life or, as they put it, need?)

Prayer is a beautiful thing between you and whoever or whatever you think of as God or your higher power. I am a big believer in prayer, and if you like praying, keep on doing it. The law of attraction can fit right into your already established prayer routine.

Prayer is similar to the asking element in the law of attraction. Don't tell God or your higher power about what you don't want. Tell him what you do want. I also recommend cutting out "I need this" and "I need that" and focusing on asking for the things or actions that will take you to a better place in your life.

A Prayer from Meg Made a Difference

To illustrate this point, I'm going to share the story of a friend of mine, a single mother of three who was struggling financially, whom we'll call Meg. She didn't receive any child support or help from her children's father, and she was running herself ragged trying to make ends meet. She prayed daily, asking for relief from the stress in her life. In her prayers, she acknowledged that she may not be deserving, and other people needed things more than she did, but maybe some financial relief could come into her life.

She asked all of her relatives to pray for her as well. She said, "Please, just pray that I won't always be so broke!" She said her prayers were never answered; she guessed she did not deserve to be happy and her lot in life must always be to suffer.

After applying the law of attraction to the way she prayed, things began to change. Instead of praying that she would never be poor again, she asked that she would be financially secure. Instead of saying she was not deserving and that other people needed things more than she did, she just eliminated those thoughts altogether.

Then she went back to her relatives and asked them to visualize her happy and financially stable. She asked them to keep praying for her but without using any negative terminology. So, they prayed that she would come into extra money and be happy. Within a month, her life turned around. Her ex-husband suddenly started to pay child support, and she got an unexpected raise at work. Now when she prays, she shows great gratitude. And she says that when she prays about the future, she always uses positive emotion instead of negative. And she says there is no crying during her prayers, only joy, as she knows her prayers will not only be heard, but answered.

Weighing the Praying

Often when prayers are not answered with what they want, folks will say it wasn't meant to be, or God had other plans.

There is a correlation here between the law of attraction and that emotional directional system I talked about earlier. Remember when I said that if there is something you want but it doesn't feel right or doesn't really make you happy, you may not get it? That's because the request is backed up with doubtful or weak emotion. The universe (a phrase that incorporates the vibrational motion of God) recognizes that wishy-washy attitude, and so does God. So, before you ask anything of either entity, invest your intent and positive emotion into the request. You can't receive if you don't believe it's what's best for you.

Before praying for something you want or think you want, use the same method you would with the law of attraction to determine whether it's worth asking for: does this feel right for you? Will this truly make you happy?

Some people are confused about combining prayer with the law of attraction. But here's how I see it: the first element of the law of attraction is asking. If you feel comfortable doing this in the form of prayer, then go right ahead. But then again, I know some very religious and spiritual people who keep the two separate. See how you feel about it and then make that decision for yourself. If you're comfortable, then the combined force of your spirituality and the law of attraction could pack a powerful wallop (in a good way). But you can't force it. God and the universe will feel that reluctance from you, and you can expect no response to your request.

Can Asking Come Back to Bite Me?

Remember: the law of attraction is the universal law, and a universal law doesn't suddenly change its orbit. It's consistently there whether you know how to work with it or not. You are always creating and receiving.

If you think using the law of attraction to attract good things can somehow suddenly reverse and make your life miserable, it can't. And it doesn't matter what or how much you ask for and receive. The universe listens; it doesn't keep score. It doesn't say, "Wow, I've been giving Jane a lot of great things lately. It's time to send her a real zinger!" These things only happen when you expect them to (and thereby attract them).

If you begin to attract what you want, you might get nervous because you are not used to success or so much joy in your life. Expressions like "all good things come to an end," should be launched into the galaxy in a space capsule. This just isn't true. All good things can remain in your life for as long as you allow them. So, keep allowing them!

How many times have you said or heard others say, "This is too good to be true! Something is bound to go wrong!"

Well, what's going wrong is that kind of thinking.

If things are too good to be true, you'd better redefine the word *true*. Because the truth is you can have it all.

Of course, the idea of "having it all" differs from person to person. It could mean a small home with a good job and a good relationship. It could mean a mansion with no job and so much money you don't have time to spend it. And to others, it may mean being healthy.

However you define it, it's okay to allow or to receive things that make you feel good. Don't rain on your own parade by thinking something could go wrong. By worrying that you're due for sadness in your life, you will create it. Then by default, you will turn your own good luck around and wonder what happened.

CHAPTER 10

Ready, Willing, and Able

In Chapter 3, I introduced you to the basic elements of the law of attraction: asking, believing, and receiving. In order for you to use this principle to your benefit, you have to concentrate on all three aspects; otherwise, you're going to hit some roadblocks. And within these elements, there are some specific skills—like asking for help and listening to your inner source—that also need to be mastered for best results.

Think of the whole process like this: A teenager needs help with his math, so his parents bring in a tutor to help him. The kid thinks "Great! This guy knows everything, so I'm so going to get an A!" The teenager goes so far as to ask his tutor for help with specific areas of math and does some half-hearted assignments to show that he's doing his part. But he doesn't listen to the answers his tutor gives, and therefore, his homework doesn't turn out even close to how the teen expects. When he doesn't get the A in the class, he can't understand what went wrong!

Can you see yourself in this scenario, even a little? You have to plug in to the universe on all kinds of different levels to get what you're looking for. I'll help clear up what's expected of you in this chapter.

Mastering Communications with Your Energy Source

You are in control of your own life. If you don't like your life, you can change it by paying more attention to your inner self or energy source, but only if you're truly in touch with that source and what it's capable of doing for you.

Too often, I see people embrace the law of attraction, become proficient at using it, and start to believe that they're achieving great things all on their own. They forget that they're cocreating their reality with the universe! These people tend to lose their focus and intent and then go into a spiral of negativity when they think the law of attraction is no longer working for them.

Leave Your Ego at the Door

Don't ever lose sight of the entire process. Skipping segments—such as asking yourself if this feels right in your gut or inner being or feeling gratitude for what you have and for what you are receiving—can start to unravel all of the powerful work you're doing!

Having confidence and believing in your requests is great—these are necessary elements in using the law of attraction successfully. But after you've had a few successes, you might feel as though you're a lightning rod of sorts, attracting wonderful things without effort or help. You may come to believe that you've somehow transformed yourself into a receiving chamber of all good things and forget that you've had assistance from a little thing called the universe.

Sometimes people lose sight of the "ask, believe, and receive" formula. They may just do the asking—briefly—and forget about whether it feels right to ask for this particular thing in the first place! They get a little cocky because they know they can tap into the universal energy to achieve whatever it is they want. There's no compassion for others, just a point of view that says, "Hey, the universe wants me to be happy! I can't help it if other people are miserable!"

Keep in mind that you are cocreating with the source of all things, whether you call that your inner being, God, or the man in the moon. In other words, you're not accomplishing all of these good things on your own! Granted, as you proceed it will become easier for you, and you will get in touch with your inner source faster, but you're still working *with* the universe.

How to Blow It with the Energy Source

In Chapter 5, we talked about your emotional guidance system as defined by authors Esther and Jerry Hicks. Let's not let that guidance system live a lonely and solitary life, sitting by the phone and waiting for you to call. *Use it.* Check in with it! This is an inner voice that tells you what feels good and what doesn't, so you can move in the direction of the things you want.

Here's an example of what happened to a dear friend of mine who we'll call Ms. C. She was leaving Florida to start a new life in North Carolina. She'd only been to Charlotte, North Carolina, a couple of times, but she felt hopeful about the area and the prospect of living and working there. What transpired during the course of her trip is a wonderful example of the inner voice that exists inside all of us and how important it is to acknowledge what it's saying! I share this with you because she wanted to help others avoid making the same mistake she did. Her story gave me a heads-up not to forget about our intuition that talks to us every moment of everyday. Here's Ms. C's story, in her own words:

> As I drove out of Sarasota, north on I-75, about 40 minutes into my journey I came to my first crossroad, a decision as to which direction—which road— would take me out of Florida and to my destination the quickest. I could have simply continued straight on the interstate, which would be the obvious way to go. But as I approached the split where I-4 takes you to I-95 through Orlando, at the last moment, I decided to head east toward Orlando. Not a moment later, as traffic slowed to a snail's pace and then to a dead halt, I was asking myself what on Earth I'd been thinking. I knew morning traffic would be at its peak. I-4 has an inadequate number of lanes to support the heavy traffic that travels this popular route. Moments earlier, I had been making wonderful time, clipping right along, feeling happy and free, knowing that I had made the right decision to leave and begin a new chapter in my life. I recall thinking I could make the 10-hour journey in one day. And now, just one wrong turn made me start to question everything.

Literally trying to keep my gaze looking forward toward the horizon, I noticed an orange-pink ball of fire rising in front of me: the sun. I had not witnessed a sunrise in ages. I was totally overcome with joy and a sense of peace, a tingling from the top of my head to tip of my toes—my usual indication that Spirit is with me and has ordained the choice—the moment. Turning east was exactly the direction I needed to be traveling in. Like the sudden and gentle appearance of the sun, simultaneously I began to hear in my mind and sing out loud the song by George Harrison "Here Comes the Sun," with its reassuring lyrics that promise everything will be all right. My body became electrified. Spirit was speaking to me. Suddenly and gently, I had confirmation that everything was all right. I remember the profound effect it had on my psyche, my soul.

I was so moved that in the moment, as traffic began to move, I thanked Spirit and asked her to pick a song for me that would indicate to me when I would be in the right place upon my arrival in Charlotte. Although I had booked a hotel, it was not set in stone.

Stopping several times to nap, several hours passed, and by that time I had forgotten all about the request I had made of Spirit. But as I was driving through Columbia, South Carolina, I heard my inner guidance system ask, "How can the universe play you a song if you keep listening to National Public (talk) Radio?" At that moment, I remembered my earlier request and randomly pressed the radio button and a station came on with an unusual variety of music. Still a long way from Charlotte, time passed, and I once again completely forgot about the request. I was driving on I-77 toward the city of Charlotte, and it was nearing the 5 o'clock hour, and traffic began to thicken. Again, as my car slowed to a snail's pace and I began to wonder where my exit would be, a song began to play over the radio that stunned me (in a good way). I distinctly recall looking at the overhead sign that read *Tyvola* as I was hearing—what else?—"Here Comes the Sun".

I felt the urge to get off at that exit, but I went against my inner guidance system and continued on to the hotel where I had booked a room for a week.

The fact that I kept driving didn't feel right to me at all. When I got to the hotel I had booked, I was highly disappointed. There were no rooms available because I had arrived a day ahead of schedule. I left the hotel and drove around looking for a place to stay. Every hotel in the area felt wrong, as did the entire neighborhood, but with few hotels providing weekly/monthly rates, choices were seemingly limited. I went back to my original hotel, and by chance, there had been a cancellation for the night, but the room wasn't clean. I was told to come back in two hours to check in. Everything was going wrong, the path suddenly seemed difficult, the way was not smooth, and I could not understand how I could have experienced such validation in the form of a song and the resulting elation and then experience such a series of upsets. Even the restaurant I chose that night was disappointing—the food was terrible!

Exhausted, I went back to the hotel and checked in and was again disappointed. Once I got past the bad smell of the room and the questionable neighborhood, I relaxed … for a few minutes. I was tired and questioning why nothing seemed to make sense since the song had played. Why had I experienced such positive signs (the sunrise, the song, and the very same song upon arriving in the Charlotte area) when the evening had held nothing but frustration for me? That night I hardly slept. Having left on a financial shoestring, I could not afford too many mistakes. I was thinking that I may have made a poor decision to move, and I was quite preoccupied with negative thoughts.

I spoke to my friend Diane on the telephone and she encouraged me to pack up and find another hotel. With little concern for finances, I quickly checked out and searched a hotel directory for a place that offered a monthly rate, which brought me to an extended-stay hotel … at the Tyvola exit.

What is the ultimate lesson to be learned from Ms. C's experience? She sums it up nicely: "All that really was required was for me to listen to my inner radar and move through life moment by moment. And if we *seemingly* make a mistake, it's all right." You can *always* turn things around!

Try this exercise: without dwelling on negative things from the past, take a few minutes to see if you can recall any incidences where you had a feeling something was right or wrong and you didn't follow your inner self talking to you. Were there opportunities for you to turn the situation around sooner? Why didn't you?

Bookmark those episodes in your memory (or even take some time to journal about them) as a reminder to always follow your instincts!

Don't Be Your Own Worst Enemy

Always keep a few things in mind when thinking in terms of communication with your energy source:

♦ You are trying to align yourself through positive vibrations; not-so-positive and doubtful thoughts have no room in your achievements.

♦ Challenging the source can come off as lack of belief. When you challenge it, the source sees your doubt, not your want. It doesn't punish you, but you just won't align with the vibration needed to cocreate your desire.

♦ Don't get angry just because you don't get what you want fast enough. Anger will only generate more situations for you to feel angry and might bring angry people into your life. Remember, like attracts like!

Another important part of the process is to believe that things will happen within reasonable time frames (time frames that are believable to you). And avoid thinking things like "This will take forever!" If you think it will take forever, then why are you asking? That creates doubt, and doubt, as you know, is a negative vibration.

Attracting Through a Physical Element

We all have different ways to make ourselves feel good about believing that we'll attract the things we want. Doubt gets us nowhere with the universe. However, some of us like to add a little extra punch to the method, and there is nothing wrong with that. For example, people have religious and spiritual rituals that make them feel their thoughts and wants have been heard.

Here are a few ways to incorporate physical elements:

♦ Light incense as a way of propelling your desire up toward the heavens.

♦ Light scented candles; as the smoke ascends from the flame, the soothing scent can help you relax.

- Chant using repeated lines or phrases.
- Pray to your higher power.
- Dance to create a vibration that puts you in a state of cheerfulness.
- Use drums; the rhythm may take you to an altered state where you can do the asking more easily.
- Write letters to your source and burn them, watching the smoke send up your message.
- Use a treasured object, such as a pendant, a statue, or a gemstone.

These ideas may seem superstitious or hokey to some, but if it works for you and contributes to a more powerful requesting process, consider using some of them. But don't incorporate them until you're 100 percent comfortable; otherwise, you could project a feeling of doubt, and that will get you nowhere fast!

Tips for Receiving

It would seem that if you're asking for and believing that something will come into your life, you would already be accepting of it, but that's not always the case. Sometimes we ask for things that we don't truly want. And sometimes we don't take the time to think about how our request will affect our lives. But deep down, I believe we know whether something will turn out for the best. When we're afraid of change or worried that something isn't truly in our best interest, we block the receiving process. In this section, I'll lead you through an easy way to evaluate your request from start to finish, before you ever get out of bed—and I'll give you a way to reset your request if things should go awry over the course of the day.

Morning, Noon, and Night

Visualizing your day doesn't take long, but don't try to cram it in with brushing your teeth and drying your hair (at least not at first). Set your alarm clock 5 minutes earlier than usual, so you can devote your full attention to this exercise.

After you wake up and before you get out of bed, take a few minutes to think about what you are expecting from the day and what you want to happen. Then allow yourself to visualize it. Feel the happiness and contentment of the day ahead of you.

Be deliberate in your thinking. It's not enough to simply say, "I want to have a great day!" If you know you are having a meeting with colleagues, for example, visualize a productive gathering, believing that even the guy from accounting who is always a troublemaker will be in good spirits and pleasant to deal with.

Creating a plan first thing in the morning enables you to evaluate what you're requesting and to answer the question, "Is this what I want?" Then you can decide whether you're open to allowing it. Too often, we have a vague idea of where we want the day to end up, but we're not requesting, believing, or allowing. We're just sort of along for the ride.

The Second Half

By midday, take a minute to evaluate. If things aren't going the way you wanted, visualize how the second half of the day will move in the right direction and believe that it *will* go that way! It may take a while for you to believe that you *can* plan the way your day is going to go, so if at first you don't succeed, try to increase your confidence. The positive vibe you put out with this belief will increase the likelihood of having the afternoon of your dreams.

Spend a few minutes (that's all it takes!) at lunch visualizing the second half of your day. Start by focusing on the small things. Perhaps you don't want that certain customer to come into the workplace that day, or you don't want the phone to ring as much as usual. And as I mentioned earlier, even though these are things that you don't want, rephrase them in terms of what you *do* want. For example, picture your workplace *without* that particular customer. Visualize a peaceful, productive afternoon where you're making lots of headway in your work and are mercifully liberated from phone calls, distracting emails, and the like. Now allow this workday into your life, instead of thinking "That would be too perfect—this peaceful afternoon could never happen!"

One Step Beyond

Although I mentioned splitting your day into morning and afternoon, you can add in the evening hours as well. Or you can step it up a bit and reprogram every time you feel things are not going your way.

If I find things are not going the way I want in the morning, I don't wait for an afternoon check-in. I stop what I am doing and switch my vibration. I try to evaluate what's gone wrong, what I want to go differently, and how I will be open to the new possibilities that the day may bring after making a new request.

So, let's say you wake up and request, "I want my boss to just leave me alone today." You believe this is possible, and you are more than willing to let this situation into your life. You arrive at work and the boss is ranting and raving at you from the minute you walk through the door. Never mind why your original request didn't work out. (I'll talk about why it may not have worked in Chapter 19.) You can switch this around by focusing on a new intent and asking something different, like "I want my boss to leave the office for the day." But think this through before you allow for it to happen—if he leaves, will this mean twice the workload or will it simply be a nice break for you?

Gratitude All Day Long

Being grateful for what you have or what you know is coming your way is very important. One of the reasons is because when you are grateful, you are allowing. You're in a good frame of mind because you are thinking of something positive you have or are doing in your life, instead of focusing on what you feel you're lacking. Also, when you are thinking of good things, there is no room for doubt, unhappiness, or discontent.

As you go through your day, make it a practice to think about the things in your life that make you happy. It's like an instant energy boost!

Author Melodie Beattie sums up the idea of giving thanks nicely:

> Gratitude unlocks the fullness of life. It turns what we have into enough and more. It turns denial into acceptance, chaos into order, confusion into clarity …. It turns problems into gifts, failures into success, the unexpected into perfect timing, and mistakes into important events. Gratitude makes sense of our past, brings peace for today, and creates a vision for tomorrow.

Be willing to allow anything of a positive nature into your life, and you may be surprised by what you find! Gratitude of this sort enables us to open our eyes to the wonderful possibilities all around us.

Why Recent Desires May Come Faster

Sometimes it just doesn't make sense to people why they have wanted, wished, and prayed for things for years and nothing happens … and then they focus on a new want and it seems to happen in the blink of an eye.

This doesn't mean that the law of attraction isn't working—in fact, this is the law of attraction in action. Let's say you've been wanting something to happen for the last year or so. Before you knew about the law of attraction, you were attracting by default. (As you know by now, you are always sending out a vibration whether you know it or not.) So, you may have been attracting what you want in one way, but undoing your hard work by having doubts about what you wanted or whether it would happen.

It's really no wonder that a new thought, fortified by your new knowledge of the law of attraction, may come faster because you don't have to override (or undo) an old vibration that you have been putting out there for heaven knows how long. You know this feeling: sometimes it's easier to start a totally new project from scratch than to try to fix something you already started (and messed up).

But don't give up on those old aspirations. You can still bring your old dreams into fruition; it just may take a tad longer. I'll go into this in detail in Chapter 19, but for now, don't get it in your head that it's going to take so long to get all of those things you've been longing for. Just understand that the newer ideas could come at lightning speed.

CHAPTER 11

Child's Play

One of the reasons it takes a while for adults to learn to use the law of attraction effectively is because we have to unlearn all of the programming we've believed in since we were children. Many of us were discouraged from shooting for the stars and were encouraged to live a very practical lifestyle instead—so as grown-ups, we tend not to believe that everything is possible. Instead, most of us believe that life follows a standard path, and we'd better not stray from that path, lest we end up living in squalor.

The good news is that it's never too late for us to change our outlook on life. The better news is that our children will never have to deprogram themselves if we teach them from the beginning that the universe is on their side.

Children and the Law of Attraction

People understand how they've cocreated their adult situations in life, but many don't understand how infants and small children have problems. How could they put out negative thinking? How do children attract ailments, anxiety, and other concerns?

Because they are open to new ideas and experiences, children are thinking and feeling all the time, even before they are born. Therefore, if they are surrounded by negative people and negative thoughts, they may absorb that negative energy and inadvertently put themselves at a disadvantage throughout their lives.

No Wonder He Cries!

It's not unusual for children to become accustomed to the energy they experience in the womb, so think positive thoughts and use positive language as much as possible when you're expecting. A pregnant woman who gets depressed often, for example, might benefit from watching funny movies if that lifts her spirits. Then again, her child may end up as a stand-up comic. (And of course, there's nothing wrong with stand-up comics.)

One mother recently told me that she was very stressed during her first pregnancy. Her husband was in the armed forces and deployed overseas, she was 1,000 miles away from her family, and she had money woes. This woman swears that her first child came out of the womb screaming and didn't stop for 6 months.

She's since had two other children; those pregnancies were peaceful compared to the first. Her other children as infants were nowhere near as difficult as the first child. "Nick would cry and cry and cry, no matter what I did for him," she says. "I read all the Zen parenting books. I tried meditation to keep myself calm. I was as calm with him as I could possibly be, and still, nothing would soothe him during those first 6 months. He's 8 years old now, and he's still very high strung, much more so than my other two kids. And I've raised them the same way." She believes that in utero, Nick absorbed the negative energy of the anxiety that she was experiencing, and it shaped his personality.

What's important to realize is that children are very sensitive to the energy surrounding them, both before and after birth. As parents, we can raise them to feel at peace or at war with the world around them. Teaching kids about universal laws is really teaching them to go with their own flow—and there's nothing wrong with that!

What If We'd Been Raised on Positive Energy?

Because the law of attraction has made a resurgence into mainstream society, it's likely that most of us weren't raised by parents who subscribed to and practiced these beliefs. But what if we had been raised to honor the universe and its energetic flow? Would we be better off today? I think so. These beliefs encourage evaluating your requests, focusing your energy on those requests, and having gratitude for everything in your life; these are habits that can only have a positive effect on one's life.

As a parent, it's your job to teach your child about life and the opportunities it has to offer. *Your* big opportunity is to consider teaching your children about the law of attraction. Think about this: if you could spare your child the irritation and heartbreak of life's most common problems (issues like negative-minded friends, dead-end jobs, draining relationships, and the like), wouldn't you do it? Now I know people say that difficult situations only make us stronger, but in my experience, I've seen difficult situations make plenty of people pessimistic and nasty.

I'm not saying that we should all float through life in a Pollyanna-like haze, but wouldn't it be nice for your children to learn about life from an optimistic view of the universe, rather than feeling as though they're pawns in life's game of chance?

Old Souls Figure It Out

Some children may catch on rather easily to the concept of attracting positive things. Because these kids tend to have a preternatural intelligence and sense of the universe, we have to wonder where those characteristics come from.

Those who believe in reincarnation (the idea that after someone dies, his or her soul lives on and eventually returns to this life in another human form to learn and grow) refer to some children (and adults for that matter) as *old souls*, meaning they have been through the life cycle several times before and have gained lots of knowledge during those lives. That's why they might have more wisdom, patience, and, in some cases, more extraordinary talent than others, or so the theory goes. So, when you see a child who's very in tune with the law of attraction, it could be that he or she has been around this universal block a time or two and is just doing what comes naturally.

Now as for those kids who have little interest in learning about the ebb and flow of universal energy, have patience with them. Don't try to lecture them on the finer points of attracting positive things. You'll have to teach by example for the most part, but there are a few other methods that you can use, and I'll discuss those throughout this chapter.

Open Vessels

The wonderful thing about children is they have not been totally jaded by the thoughts and experiences of others. And if they have, they are young enough to switch things around before more negative influences may encompass them.

The law of attraction sounds like heavy material for kids, but these days, people start teaching children some rather adult things at a very young age. Years ago, the theory was that infant and toddler brains weren't developed enough to appreciate music, letters and numbers, or reading. Educators today have a far different take on the issue: they recognize that the immature brain is ready and willing to soak up information!

Introducing the law of attraction to your child doesn't need to be a complicated, time-consuming event. It's something you can incorporate into everyday life, actually, and it's rather easy to do. I don't want your kids to feel like learning about this is a drag—it should be fun and exciting!

Learning to use the law of attraction is an empowering experience for anyone, and the earlier kids get in touch with it, the better their attitudes seem to be when life does throw them a curveball or two. This is because they know that they aren't going to fight the universe; they're going to work with it.

Plant the Seeds Now!

Before you introduce this idea into your child's psyche, it is important that *you* have a grasp on the subject and a firm belief that it is already working in your life. This is where you lead by example. When you are comfortable with the idea of living life from a positive energetic viewpoint, then you can start to involve your children.

When can you begin teaching them these principles? It's really a matter of personal preference. As I mentioned earlier, you can begin concentrating on positive thoughts as soon as you find out you're expecting. As your child grows, you have to feel the time is right to teach your child about these concepts. If the whole idea makes you uncomfortable, that means *you* aren't ready—and you can't teach this if you don't believe it wholeheartedly. Put the discussion on hold until you feel better about it.

Some parents feel that it's best to wait until their children are entering those teen years before introducing them to these ideas. I think it's best to start earlier if you are comfortable with your own beliefs.

A 13-year-old will probably logically understand that a negative attitude invites more negative energy into her life. However, few things are logical to a 13-year-old who's having a hard time socially or academically. I think it's better to head that bad attitude off at the pass by explaining these ideas to her *before* she reaches the point of hating life and everyone around her. You can do this by making the law of attraction part of your child's habits, understanding, and upbringing.

Encourage Their Dreams

When your children start telling you they want this and want that—and they will—pay attention to how you respond. Try to use positive vibes as often as possible.

Really think about how you approach certain topics. Instead of saying, "You can't eat all that candy. Sugar is really bad for you and it will make you fat," say, "Let's find a healthy snack." It's a subtle difference, but one is tainted with negative emotion and the other simply isn't. The difference down the road is the way your child learns to look at life and, in turn, use the law of attraction.

Basically, you want to create a dialogue that focuses on what she can do rather than what she can't. (More do's than don'ts, in other words.) Now I'm not suggesting that you let your child do anything she wants to do. I'm saying that there are two ways to say anything: a negative way and a positive way. For example, if your 4-year-old wants to climb the highest slide on the playground and you feel it's an injury waiting to happen, you can respond in one of two ways:

- "No way! You're going to fall and break your neck!"
- "There's a slide over here that's for kids your age."

Do you see the difference? One response is focused on what the child isn't capable of doing, and the other is focused on her abilities right here, right now. The law of attraction, remember, focuses on what is possible. You want your child to adapt that mind-set.

When your child tells you that he wants to be a firefighter or a police officer when he grows up, don't tell him what a dangerous profession it is and how you would never sleep again knowing that he was in harm's way. Tell him that these men and women do a great service for others and that it's a choice he can make when he's older. (At which point, he'll probably want to be a rock star. Remember to stay positive!)

The point is that you *have* to teach your kids the difference between right and wrong and safe and unsafe. "Don't touch the stove!" isn't necessarily a negative command—it's for his own protection, so that's an exception. But whenever the choice presents itself, try to go with the positive vibes. You'll notice a difference in your own attitude when you become proficient at this.

When to Rein Them In

There's a big difference between letting a child know that the universe is on her side and allowing her to think that she's the *center* of the universe. In the previous section, I said that it's important to teach kids the difference between right and wrong, which includes teaching them about compassion and caring about others.

If you see your child mastering the art of the law of attraction and getting everything she wants—whether those are material things or specific experiences—remind her that in the eye of the universe, no one is better than anyone else, and certainly not because of the things they have. Some people are just better than others at attracting the things they want. So, along with the basics of the law of attraction, focus on teaching your child to have a positive, caring attitude toward others. After all, kindness and compassion are positive vibrations that benefit your child *and* everyone around her!

Kid Talk

The universal law says we are here to experience fun, joy, and happiness. So, if a child feels like he is at school when he is at home, he may become a bit resistant to learning new ideas. If that's the case, then come down to his level when teaching the law of attraction. Introduce new terms slowly or hold off on the lingo altogether, opting instead to teach only the concepts of the law of attraction.

More than anything else, it's important to show your child that the law of attraction works; when you do this, he'll easily accept it as fact. If you meditate when making your requests, then by all means, meditate where your child can see you (as long as you can concentrate with your child in the room). When you do your affirmations, let him hear them loud and clear! When you make a request, do so out loud, during or after your meditation or affirmation session: "I am traveling to a conference tomorrow. I request of the universe a safe and productive trip."

Teaching by example extends to all areas of your life. If you're calm and serene at home while making your requests and focusing your energy, then strive to be calm and serene in other areas of your life. Don't, for example, make rude gestures at the person who cuts you off in traffic. Your child will have a hard time reconciling this angry person behind the wheel with the person who's been telling him to look at things from a positive point of view. Concentrate on exuding positivity at all moments, and your child will absorb your teachings without ever having a formal lesson!

Methods for Introducing Positive Energy

The origins of the law of attraction, who uses it, and which noted people from the past have used it, and all that we talked about at the beginning of the book is interesting information but not when you're 10 years old. Would you have wanted to receive that information before elementary school? Probably not.

I am appealing to, for the sake of a better expression, the interests of the average child. There are, of course, those old souls who might have a deeper interest in the origins of this concept—for them, I say go for it! Teach them everything! But for most kids, keep it simple and try not to overwhelm them.

Visual Aids Kids Can Relate To

First things first: you want to teach a young child how important it is to be in touch with her emotions. (If you recall, we talked about the importance of emotions and intent in Chapter 5.) After a while, the child will be in touch with what makes her feel happy or sad. She always knows, by nature, and that will make her asking for what she wants all the easier.

How do you teach a young child to identify her feelings of joy and sadness? Be as creative as you want, but I suggest you find something that children can look at with what they think of as up and down or positive and negative.

Get a piece of poster board, a blackboard, or anything you can draw on. Draw a happy smiley face on one side and a sad frowning face on the other. Ask her which face makes her feel happier.

Then start to ask her a series of questions, and tell her to point to the face that shows how she feels after you ask her each question.

Some suggestions for questions are as follows:

- When I say you can't go out and play, how do you feel?
- When you are at school and the teacher gives you a lot of homework, how do you feel?
- What does it feel like when you open your birthday presents?
- When a kid at school makes fun of you, how do you feel?
- How do you feel when you have your favorite dinner?
- When you see or hear people fighting, how do you feel?
- When you are playing your favorite video game, how do you feel?
- When you're at Grandma's, or at your best friend's house, or tucked into bed—any safe place—what does that feel like?

Obviously, you can customize this list to include things that are personal to your child, like her favorite toy, her least favorite food, etc.

Don't be concerned about teaching your child to recognize sad feelings. You're not going to turn your kid into a depressed little soul; you're simply teaching her to differentiate between emotions so she can use positive energy to her benefit.

More Happy Faces

The next step is to ask your child if he would like to have more happy faces than sad faces. Attached to his yes answer should be some excitement and intrigue because he assumes you are going to attempt to teach him how to be happier, or you wouldn't be asking the question.

- Ask him what feels better, the word *yes* or *no*? What gives him that smiley-face feeling?
- If he had to pick a word that would make him choose the smiley face, is it *do* or *don't*?
- Which two-word set makes him feel better: *I can* or *I can't*?

The key here is to have your child acknowledge which set of words makes him feel happier—but *you* have to carry through with using the positive words each day. This isn't an overnight process, but it's also not a difficult adjustment to make. It just takes effort.

Tell your child you have a magic method, a secret, or a special message from those who learned this "happy method" long ago that changes every frowning face into a smiling face.

When children are learning to spell, you ask them to use certain words in a sentence, so you know they understand what they are spelling. We're going to use a similar method to give your child an understanding that certain words bring back certain feelings that make him feel bad.

Tell him to use the words *can't, don't, no,* and *not* in as many sentences as he wants, and to use each word at least once.

Have him write it down, as it will make more of an impression. He may come up with things like this:

- My mother tells me *don't* forget to brush my teeth.
- You *can't* play with electronic games until your homework is done.
- I *don't* want you to come in here with muddy shoes.
- *No* playing ball in the house.
- You will *not* go to your friend's house until your room is clean.

Before you know it, you will be buying extra paper and the process will have begun. When he is done writing, ask him again to draw a smiley face or a frowning face on what he wrote. Right about now, you'll have a bunch of frowny little faces looking at you, but don't fret. It's all part of learning to use positive language.

Don't Say Don't

Just as we are trying to train ourselves as adults to look at what we want and don't want, the same goes for the little ones we are trying to enlighten. Remind them that saying *don't, can't, not,* and *no* make them sad. By changing those words to *do, can, will,* and *yes,* they will start to have more smiles on their own faces.

The first thing children need to do when they catch themselves using those words and feeling bad is to think about a specific phrase: "Don't tell me what you don't want; tell me what you do want." As I said earlier, adults need to do this, too. The difference is that adults' needs are usually more life altering; kids are fortunate to be practicing this method on relatively minor issues like homework and sports. (These issues aren't minor to them, of course, but you know what I mean.)

So, have your child look back to those *don't* sentences and figure out how to change them:

- *Negative:* My mother tells me *don't* forget to brush my teeth.
  Positive: Remember to brush your teeth.

- *Negative:* You *can't* play until your homework is done.
  Positive: When your homework is done, you *can* go play.

- *Negative:* I *don't* want you to come in here with muddy shoes.
  Positive: Take off your shoes before you come in the house.

- *Negative: No* playing ball in the house.
  Positive: Play ball outside.

- *Negative:* You will *not* go to your friend's house until your room is clean.
  Positive: After you clean your room, you can go to your friend's house.

If they don't get this idea, you have to help them a bit. For example, some kids might use a different negative word to describe the same thing. Your child might rewrite "You can't play till your homework is done," as "Don't play until your homework is done." Obviously, this defeats the purpose, so help her come up with a phrase that uses more positive language.

Stick with this what-makes-you-feel-better verbiage with younger children. As they get older, you can replace it by asking them to identify what kind of emotion, vibration, or vibe they're feeling.

Keep in mind, our children have the potential to change their futures to a more positive state of being! It's easy to introduce the law of attraction into everyday life. Even if you don't do any formal teaching, do try to remain positive and believe that anything is possible—that attitude will transfer to your children.

A Weekly Achievement Board

Another great tool for teaching positive energy is a weekly achievement board. We have them for all types of things, so why not use one when we catch ourselves using words like *don't*, *won't*, and *can't?*

Of course, the whole point of this is to focus on the positive, so instead of charting the number of negative words your kid has used, have him note how many times he started to think about what he didn't want and replaced that thought with what he did want.

See how well this works. You don't want your child obsessing over every single thought, so make that very clear. But if a major event occurs—like your son started to say to himself, "I can't pass this test," and he caught herself and changed his thinking—then that's definitely worthy of a star on the achievement board!

Fun Family Meetings: What Have You Attracted This Week?

If everyone is game, you can put together a weekly or monthly family meeting to talk about how well everyone's doing with positive thoughts. You can talk about your desires, what you're asking of the universe, whether you're having a hard time believing and allowing—whatever feels comfortable.

School-aged kids might be really into correcting your language during this teaching process ("I heard you say you *can't* make it to the meeting because of your sister's baby shower! I thought we're supposed to be using positive words!"), so instead of responding to your little critic every day, you can suggest that she bring up her concerns at the meeting. This helps keep everyone on track and also eliminates negative energy in the household, which only attracts more negative energy.

If your kids don't feel comfortable with a weekly meeting, stick with the achievement board or simply ask them how they are doing with this process once in a while. Whichever method you use is fine; just make sure you're investing quality into it.

It's important to keep this process fun. If your child doesn't seem to have the desire to do this or has trouble catching on, try again at a later date. Or when she starts complaining about how terrible her life is, reiterate something like this: "Remember you told me how you are happier when you think about what you want rather than what you don't want? Do you want to try again?"

Let's not forget—oops—I mean, *let's remember* that everyone has a different time that's right for them, including children. Present this idea slowly, and keep it light. But if you keep using the law, the next thing you know your children will be right up there with you creating positive and joyful things in their lives.

PART 4

People, Places, and Specific Intents

Many people turn to the law of attraction because they have very specific wants in their lives—better health, more money, a companion, and so on. Are there ways to make sure your specific requests are heard and answered? There sure are—and you'll read all about them in these chapters.

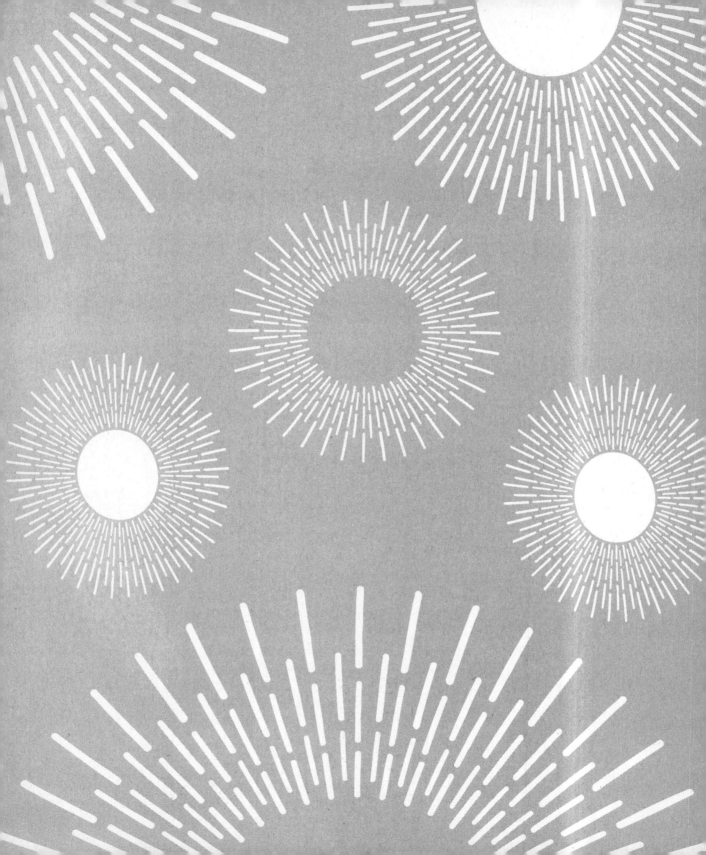

CHAPTER 12

An Apple a Day and Positive Intent

"Without your health, you don't have anything." I'm sure you have uttered those words before or at least have heard them said. If you're in ill health, you no doubt know the value of feeling great; if you're in good health, take some time to consider how fortunate you are. Without good health, how will you be able enjoy the things you are going to create for yourself?

When talking about health, know that mental health is also a part of well-being. So many people have had miracle stories of recovery, and others feel cheated because they have not. But there's enough power in the universe to improve everyone's health, so there's no reason for anyone to be left feeling resentful of others' good fortune. Having said that, I must add that there are some definite methods for focusing on better physical and emotional health; I'll tell you about them in this chapter.

Keep the Good Health Flowing

Author Claude M. Bristol says, "Every person is the creation of himself, the image of his own thinking and believing. As individuals think and believe, so they are."

Thinking "I am healthy, and grateful for my good health," should be a regular part of your daily routine. If you are ill, thoughts of becoming healthy should be your daily focus. Again, it's important to dwell on the positive possibilities. Lying in bed thinking "Why me, why me, why me?" will do you no good. Sending out that negative vibration will ensure that you get more negativity back from the universe.

Sometimes your mind and the law of attraction work like an advertising scheme. If you say it often enough, you start to take notice and believe it. And once you can believe it, you most certainly can allow it!

"I Never Get Sick"

Every day, take the time to acknowledge your good health and to show gratitude for it, even if you're not well at the moment. Say, "I am always healthy." Close your eyes and visualize your health as a glowing orb around you, if you like. Think of it as a force field that's always present to protect you.

When common illnesses come to pass, don't get so irritated or angry that your whole week is going to be ruined—that only makes matters worse. If you get a sniffle, don't panic and focus on the cold it could become. Think "This is just passing through my body right now," and then don't think about it anymore than you absolutely must. In other words, don't moan and groan and text your friends to describe every symptom of your congestion. Blow your nose, wash your hands, and get on with your day, focusing on something other than your stuffy sinuses.

Envision a Better You

Continuing on in good health is easy for someone who is already healthy, just as staying at a healthy, stable weight is easier than having to lose 30 pounds and then trying to keep it stable. So, for those of you who already have physical health concerns, I understand that it's going to take a lot of effort to focus on something other than your pain and suffering. Try to take a moment several times a day to visualize yourself in the health you want to be in. Look at old pictures of yourself when you were healthier (as long as they don't make you sad). Can you remember how your days went, the things you were able to do, the joy you found in those activities? Send those positive feelings to the universe, saying, "I am on my way to feeling *that* healthy again."

Because poor health can be stressful, requesting good health is a two-step process. First, you must put yourself into a relaxed state of mind, free of anxiety, anger, resentment, etc. To reach this point, I recommend deep breathing with your eyes closed. Pay close attention to your breathing—this is how you put yourself into a calm state of mind. Once you're there, you can focus on making your request, using positive language, of course.

Make Your Doctor's Job Easier

Having a healthy attitude doesn't mean you shouldn't seek medical attention if you need it. The law of attraction doesn't state that real illness doesn't exist—indeed, it does! If you need a health-care professional, go get help. While you're waiting to see the doctor or waiting for test results, think of the best possible outcome, not the worst.

It's interesting that even studies have shown that patients who pray or meditate daily, who are in happy partnerships, or who have a social network of friends and family tend to fare better when they are ill than those who don't. A positive mind-set is incredibly powerful!

I am also a firm believer in attracting the right medical professional to yourself. If you believe that your doctor is not on your same energetic plane, so to speak, then find a new doctor. Obviously, you want an intelligent and gifted physician, but you also want someone who's going to understand that you're using visualization and positive thought to heal, so that he or she can work with you. It can be a painful conflict (not to mention a counterproductive situation) when a doctor belittles your beliefs and attempts to heal yourself. So, ask the universe to guide you to the right co-healer, so that you can heal as fast as possible.

Stop Feeling Sorry for Me!

When you think you are getting sick, remind yourself that you are always healthy. As I mentioned, if you need medical attention, don't delay. But also don't feed into what others have to say to the point of becoming a hypochondriac. Someone may say, "You look a little sick today." In response you should say, "I am always healthy."

After a while people will start to believe that you are, in fact, always healthy. They'll comment to others about your amazing health, giving you and your immune system more energy, and therefore, more of a power boost from the universe!

If people already know that you have a serious illness, you may be receiving their pity, which can sure feel good sometimes, but it will hurt your recovery in the long run. *You* have to be the person who stops the pity party! Tell others to stop feeling sorry for you and to visualize you happy and healthy. Ask them never to talk about your health issues with other people; when friends and family members chat about your ill health, they are sending out a vibration that you are ill, which only helps you stay that way. This is *unintentional alignment*, which occurs when others talk about your problems, thus giving the problems a voice and a power they would not have otherwise.

Here's one thing I do to help when my friends are ill: I never send serious get-well cards—you know, the ones that are heavy with concern. I send something with a funny picture, a randy joke, or both. Easier yet, send a funny text or email. They say laughter is the best medicine, after all, and I want my sick friends and relatives to feel light-hearted and smiley so that they can send a vibe out to the universe that says, "I have some positive energy in me still!"

And please, never say to someone, "I am so sorry you're sick." Rather say, "I'm looking forward to the time we can go to lunch (or go fishing, or play tennis, etc.) again." What would you rather hear from someone?

When it comes to kids' illnesses, always have a positive perspective. Have you ever said to someone something like, "Oh, my little Tony is my sickly one"? Don't do that—to him or to yourself! Instead, think—and say—"My kid is getting stronger as he gets older, and I'm glad he's staying in good health these days." If you sink to that level of saying, "Tony's sick again! He's just so frail!" then that child is being programmed to remain sick. And whenever a little sniffle comes along, Tony will grab onto that negative vibe, send it out to the universe, and end up bedridden.

If you recognize yourself as a parent who labels a child this way, shake it off. You didn't know about the law of attraction before—but now that you do, change your outlook and your comments. A healthier attitude for you may mean a healthier child, too.

Loneliness Hurts

I once heard that the number one illness in the United States is loneliness. In fact, according to recent research, more Americans than ever before report feeling isolated, with fewer than three social contacts to confide in.

Mental illness can be one side effect of loneliness and can even be worse than physical illness because you lose all perspective as to when and if things can ever improve, with or without the help of the universe. Someone who is mentally ill may not even have the energy to focus on asking the universe for help, which means that things usually spiral downward, downward, downward, until it seems as though it's impossible to get back up.

Nowadays, we all have access to the internet, and many of us connect with others in cyberspace. However, doing so has its downside as well, in that online chitchatting is not really a substitute for face-to-face relationships. Think about using the internet to join an in-person volunteer or hobby group, and thereby attract friends into your life. If you are not the outgoing type, join a class where you learn something. Maybe you will find a like-minded friend despite yourself!

Too Much Solitude Leads to Ill Health

Some people really do enjoy solitude. In a sense, as a writer, I am perfectly happy to be alone in front of my computer, eating mashed potatoes and gravy, wearing an old T-shirt, and not worrying about my unshaven legs. Shampoo? I've heard of that. Although I enjoy my alone time, I find that after a while it can become lonely.

Some folks find that having too much solitude is a disheartening experience. There's no one to connect with, to share opinions with, or even to laugh with. When common aches and pains come a knockin', as they always do, they seem worse than they really are because you have nothing else to focus your attention on. The negative energy takes hold and starts sprinting away with your health!

If this happens to you, remember that you are never really alone. Don't feel bad about wanting companionship. As a species, humans are social creatures, constantly on the lookout to make some sort of personal connection. Think about it: we must be programmed to be that way or the species couldn't carry on!

You are a part of this great big universe, and if you have no one to speak to, you can always speak to your power source. Ask it to provide you with a human companion, and describe his or her characteristics. Visualize yourself and your companion whiling away weekend or evening hours together, just happy to have one another's company. I'll talk more about attracting relationships in Chapter 13.

Purrrfect

Another way to abate loneliness is to attract the perfect pet into your life. To be sure, pets give you a reason to get up in the morning and a reason to come home at night. They also give you plenty of love and affection. That's why you should make them a part of your daily visualizing and meditative thoughts. When concentrating on your own good health, include your pet being happy and healthy, too. You don't want a pet's ill health to bring you down.

Research has shown that pets help lower blood pressure, increase general happiness, and decrease depression, all of which can increase your health and will, in turn, increase your happiness level even more. You'll be caught in an upward spiral of positive thought, positive interaction, and positive movement!

Some people hear "the perfect pet" and think of a Standard poodle or an English sheep dog. Take some time to think about the perfect pet for *you*. Is your ideal pet affectionate, easy to care for, active, cuddly, big, small, scaly? Unfortunately, when folks don't take the time to think these things through, they often end up with a pet who's irritating at best and a complete nuisance at worst. This exacerbates feelings of loneliness and frustration, especially because the person winds up feeling like she's tried and failed to make a basic connection. The negative downward spiral continues.

See a Full Life

You may not particularly like animals and maybe you don't want a mate, either. If that's the case, you can still attract a full life. Think of volunteer work, making friends in a group instead of on an individual basis. Some people want to keep busy but don't want to get too involved with one person, platonic or otherwise. There are social networking groups you can get involved with from home, hobbies, internet games with other players, and many other ways you can fight the lonely bug, increase your positive energy, and improve your health while you're at it.

Use the law of attraction to ask for ideas that will enable you to choose some interesting things to fill your life with. If you're focused on this task, the universe will start to drop hints, so pay attention. You might suddenly get a flyer from the local art guild. Then the next thing you know, the rain starts pouring and detours you into a local art shop. Then you start seeing advertisements for art lessons. Before you know it, the law of attraction has delivered to you a new hobby: making ceramic candy dishes.

Stories of Recovery and Healing

I love real-life stories because there's just no better way to capture the excitement, passion, and gratitude of life-changing events. I have found a few accounts of healing that I hope you find inspirational for attracting well-being.

I Only Thought I Was Sick

Ken was a 50-year-old furniture salesman. He wasn't what you would call thrilled with his job, but he was what he called "happy enough." Ken used to cough all the time for no known reason. His doctors thought he might have a little allergy to dust or something minor. His father had died of lung cancer, so he was always in fear of getting the same thing. He never smoked, but he dreaded that this could be his fate, especially as he got older.

The doctors took blood, did chest X-rays, and found nothing. Still, Ken used to tell his wife that he was sure he was going to develop cancer. It ran in the family he told her, and with every passing year, his turn was getting closer and closer. He planned for it. He thought about how much time he might have to take off from work for surgery, chemotherapy, radiation treatments, etc. He said, "As long as they catch it early, I might survive."

This went on for years. One day he started coughing due to a cold. He immediately went to the doctor and wanted to know "the truth" so he could prepare himself and his family. The truth was he had a cold.

Both of Ken's parents had died by this time, but his dear old grandmother was still alive. Although she was elderly and not in the best health herself, she could see that he was obsessing over this cancer. Although she didn't call it the law of attraction, she knew that people usually got exactly what they expected, and she was determined not to let this happen to her grandson.

One day she called Ken and outright lied to him, saying all this time she had not told him the truth. She told him his father died from unknown causes; she and Ken's mother never wanted Ken to smoke, so they had told him the cause of death had been lung cancer. Ken was alarmed. He wanted to investigate further, but his grandmother convinced him that it wouldn't do him any good. Ken's father had died 30 years earlier, and those records wouldn't still be around, she said. (This raises the question: is it alright to lie to someone, or does it create a negative vibe? In my opinion, in extreme instances such as this, the end justifies the means; if you have to fib to someone to save him from himself, then so be it.)

To continue Ken's story: after the call from his grandmother, Ken never worried about lung cancer again. He quit his so-so job and got a job doing what he really liked, which was tending bar. Here's the kicker: he had never become a bartender because he'd been worried about the smoky environment accelerating the (imagined) dormant lung tumor that he assumed was waiting to blossom into cancer. He eventually opened up his own bar, and now lives a healthy and happy life, free of coughing. Ken eventually did find records with the cause of his father's death, but he was already so content with how his life had turned out, he didn't care. Now that he believes in the law of attraction, he is trying to attract another bar in Canada for his brother to run. Cheers!

I'm Walking

Douglas is 88 years young and lives alone, but is looking for a girlfriend. (His 85-year-old wife passed away two years ago.) He kayaks, plays tennis, and loves to dance.

When he was 70, he was told he would never walk again because of a degenerative illness. Well, Douglas is a stubborn old goat, to coin a phrase. He simply didn't believe the medical tests or diagnosis. As he puts it, he went along with the doctors, did what they said, and nothing happened. They could not figure out why he was still walking. They thought that maybe the worst of the affliction would hit him all of a sudden instead of gradually, the way it affected most people. He told me he just always thought about how he loved to be active and wouldn't let any thoughts about not walking to enter his mind.

Is Douglas a miracle? No, not really. He just kept visualizing himself as a happy, active person instead of worrying about the crippled person he was *supposed* to be becoming. He ended our interview by saying, "And let the readers know that I don't need Viagra, either." Oh, my!

Dora's a "Loser"

Dora, a nurse, was overweight, had high blood pressure, and was borderline diabetic. She was always embarrassed about being in the medical field and being in such ill health. She claimed that her problems were due to her thyroid, until a doctor told her differently. Then she said it was depression, but she was actually quite a happy person, aside from her weight. Dora took motivational classes, read books, bought pills, joined weight-loss groups, and still, the weight hung on to her, as if for dear life.

At that point, she simply started to say, "It's hereditary." This is not uncommon. Too often, people hear that there's a hereditary condition in their family and assume their future is set in stone. "Hereditary" isn't the same as saying, "You are soooo going to end up with all of the same problems your relatives have had." Attract better health than your relatives! Now whether her family was obese and diabetic, I don't know, but at that point, it was like she had given up and surrendered to her DNA.

Then she discovered the law of attraction and went to work. She pictured herself thinner as she ate a bag of chips and salsa. She wrote down the weight she wanted to be after she polished off the last of the fettuccine Alfredo, which she believed shouldn't go to waste. (It was just *so* good!) So, she ate and asked, ate and believed, and ate and allowed. I know you think you know what I am going to write, that we need to act along with the asking. But I can't do that this time. Dora started losing weight while still eating the same things she used to. *"What?!"* you're thinking. I was even a bit shocked. She went to the doctor to see if she had a tapeworm, or if she was ill. She was just as healthy as before. In fact, she dropped 2 pounds a week for almost 3 months straight with the exceptions of a few plateaus.

Now I am not implying that you should eat more and not take action if weight loss is your goal, but a story is a story, and I find this an interesting case of the law of attraction coming into play. Dora really believed. She said nothing in her life had worked to improve her health … except for the law of attraction.

Dora is now down to her goal weight and has slowly made improvements in the overall quality of the food she eats. If she could do this with the kind of handicaps she was facing, I think that you can certainly do it, too, no matter how overweight or how many weight-related issues you're dealing with. Again, I don't want to use Dora's eating habits as an example of anything other than how strong the law of attraction is and how it can override any seemingly impossible circumstances in your life. I still recommend healthy eating and asking to attract a program or system that will work for you. Yet we can't ignore the story of Dora.

I Don't Have Time for Cancer

When Pearl, who lived in a small town in Idaho, was diagnosed with colon cancer, she was not surprised. She had been having all sorts of personal problems for quite some time, and this seemed to be a fitting finale to years of trouble. She was not a woman of means, and her husband had just retired and had his own set of medical problems. Her son, Frank, who was in his twenties, had difficulties finding work, and Pearl had to support him most of the time.

When her diagnosis came in, the doctor told her she needed chemotherapy, which would not allow her to remain in her current job. With no medical insurance and virtually no income, times were difficult, to say the least. She was the one who should have been taken care of, but instead she found herself caring for her sick husband. Cancer or not, she felt it was her duty to show him the love and support he had given her when he was well. And Frank, he was a nice-enough guy, but he was not the most motivated or nurturing person.

So, Pearl found a way to get a little part-time work that wasn't straining, and after work she had to cook, clean, and do laundry for her two fellows. Every time I talked to her, she had a new problem and was dwelling on the fact that her husband and son were no help. She said she did not have time to take care of herself because it was "all about them." But interestingly enough, she went through chemotherapy with the weight of the world on her shoulders and is cancer-free today.

Did she practice the law of attraction to become cancer-free? Not really, as she was focusing on the lack of help from her son and husband. With that said, what she *didn't* do—by default—was to think about herself, her condition, and whether she would make it through or not. She shifted her illness away from her consciousness and focused on other things. She had help from other loving family members and friends who were worth their weight in gold. They would often advise her to start focusing only on herself. But according to the law of attraction, by not giving the cancer much thought, she moved through it. Had she been lying in a chaise lounge being waited on by her husband and son, contemplating her illness, she may have been worse off because she would have been feeding the cancer more energy.

Yes, she could have kept visualizing herself healthy, but that didn't work for her. She was an active person and needed to occupy her thoughts with something else. Unfortunately, most of her thoughts were negative, but because they weren't focused on her illness, the only repercussions were that her son and husband continued not to help out. But as time went on, Pearl gained strength and started focusing on what she wanted in her life instead of what she didn't want. Even if you have nothing but time to focus on yourself and your illness, try to think of other things. If you're well enough, travel, visit others, or volunteer at something that isn't too taxing. Putting your problems into perspective often leads to a certain amount of gratitude, which improves your chances of healing.

Now Pearl is cancer-free, her son is working and helping his parents out financially, and her husband is telling jokes like he used to. The family is intact, healthy, and happy.

The law of attraction can work in many ways to leave you happier, more focused, and healthier than you've felt in years. And because it's 100 percent free of charge—no copays, no referrals, no precertification needed—you can put it to good use in your health regimen today. It's worked for others; it will work for you, too!

CHAPTER 13

Your Relationships: Cocreators of Your Reality

Each one of us has relationships of all different natures. There are those *amore* relationships, which translates from Italian as "romance, passion, and fascination." Then we have *agape* relationships, which translates from Greek as "unconditional love, be it of family members or romantic partners." An amore-agape relationship with a partner is probably the best, because you may have it all in the emotional department, to say the least.

Unfortunately, we can wind up in relationships where we've fallen in love way before the other person has. Even worse, the other person may not know, care, or want a relationship with us at all!

Did you attract that type of heartbreak? Is there anything you can do to get yourself on a better path? Better yet, is there a way to make someone return your feelings of admiration? In this chapter, I'll take a look at relationships of every sort and talk about ways to improve them … or to let go of them.

Romance

Sometimes when people hear about the law of attraction, they assume it must be about romantic relationships. We tend to associate the word *attraction* with finding a hot date or attracting a soul mate. When I told friends and acquaintances that I was writing a book about the law of attraction, I can't tell you how many people told me they were willing to share their love stories of happiness and of woe. And although romance is a small part of what we attract in life, its power can be inspiring or devastating. In other words, its effect on us can make it seem as though romance is the only thing that matters.

Blind Love

There he or she is, the man or woman of your dreams. This person is everything you wanted—or should I say everything you attracted? Whether you realize it or not, you put a lot of intention into the kind of relationship you want in your life. You put great emotion behind it, which catapults it into those fluffy pink clouds where your head currently spends its days and evenings. "To be in love is merely to be in a state of perceptual anesthesia—to mistake an ordinary young man for a Greek god or an ordinary young woman for a goddess," H. L. Mencken, twentieth-century journalist, satirist, and freethinker describes it so well. But how did you get into this state?

You aligned that love vibration with the spirit of the person who is now the master of your heart and spirit.

Now here's the really important part: your mate was looking for love at the same time you were, so you connected on the same energetic frequency. True love just can't happen if one person is allowing it and the other person isn't.

Was your newfound sweetheart specific about falling in love with someone with your characteristics and spirit? Did he not even know he was attracting you to himself? There could be a chance that you attracted each other by default, by thinking with passion and intention, "I want to fall in love." In this case, the intention was not focused on the specific sort of love interest—just on finding one.

True Love and Energy

So, you and your mate may have been working on the same vibrational signal and fell into each other's arms for the sake of being in love. What happens once that vibration dissipates and your true natures and energies come into play? Well, if the two of you have compatible energies—and by compatible, I don't mean identical—everything can work out just fine. *Complementary* is the word I'd use here; you can have positive energy and vibration and your mate can be very laid back about almost everything in life. Together, the two of you create one unit of happiness and peace. Couples who are too similar—both high energy or both low energy—sometimes run into issues because combining their energy creates either a volcano (two high energies) or a vacuum (two low energies). Your energetic levels will determine whether you and your mate have common interests and whether you can live together without losing your minds. Two low-energy partners may not get much of anything done, while two high-energy partners may criticize each other incessantly.

Now don't be afraid of change. You can give in to your partner on some issues without losing yourself in the process. But if you don't feel that your energetic combination is right, then you have gone against your inner directional finder. The reason this person came into your life may have been to open your eyes in some way and to help you find your true mate.

You Can't Begin Anew Without a Positive End

When you decide to break it off with someone who is not a good fit for you, do it with dignity, wish him or her well, and *mean* it. Bear in mind, the more negative thoughts you have during a breakup, the more negative the other person's reaction will be. She'll pick up on your negativity and give it right back to you, and *that* will hinder your ability to move on and find someone new.

For example, let's say you're breaking up with someone and she asks, "What do you think of me?" Either focus on some positive traits like, "You're kind and funny, but you're just not for me," or something neutral, such as, "I think you're a special person." The key is to keep your responses open and honest and neutral, if at all possible, so as not to attract (or send) negative energy. You might even say,

"I simply want to move on so we are both happy." That doesn't feed any vibration one way or the other.

Now on the other hand, if you think someone has fallen out of love with you and you want her back, focus on his good qualities and think about the good times. Don't put guilt on her or obsess about how he did you wrong.

Think like the wise sage Hazrat Inayat Khan, author of *Spiritual Dimensions of Psychology* and founder of Universal Sufism, who said, "The best thing is not to hate anyone, only to love. That is the only way out of it. As soon as you have forgiven those whom you hate, you have gotten rid of them. Then you have no reason to hate them; you just forget."

If your ex is on the same energetic path as you are, you will come back together. Positive thoughts and vibrations are more likely to work toward this end than negative energy is, so don't dwell on what went wrong. But as always, if the inner source is telling you it's really over, then it isn't going to work (the vibration you're putting out to the universe is weak and indecisive), so listen up and save yourself some time.

From Afar ...

Strong relationships don't come along every day. We have to allow them into our lives and so do the people we're hoping to be in relationships with; if the feelings are mutual and genuine, both parties are happy. But sometimes you may like someone, be it a business partner, a romantic partner, or a shopping buddy, and that person is just not on the same page you are. She or he is just not that into you!

That's an unrequited relationship. By definition, the word *unrequited* basically means not reciprocated. Is there any way to focus your energy and make these hesitant potential friends and lovers see how amazing, loyal, intelligent, and funny you are? Not really, but there are some things you can do to *not* make matters worse and to improve your chances of changing things for the better in the future.

Unrequited Friendships

Let's say you find a friend you really connect with. You have the same interests and have had a lot of great times together. Actually, you think you have a new best friend in this person and then ... she doesn't call you for a week, which seems like an eternity because you were speaking three times a day before. Suddenly you feel slighted, asking yourself, "What did I do? Why is she suddenly hanging out with Susie Q instead of me? They never include me in their girls' nights out!"

Yup, you can really have some feelings of rejection in such a case. What have you done to deserve this?

Just like with romantic relationships, friendships can fall apart for reasons we don't fully understand. Can you focus your intent and ask the universe to send you more good times with this person? No. You simply can't force someone to be your friend, no matter what kind of mystical tools you have in your corner. Don't try to guilt someone into giving you more attention because you are centering your thoughts on what he or she is *not* doing. Instead, try focusing your attention on making yourself a more positive-minded person. You won't believe the great results this will bring into your life!

Just in case there was some sort of misunderstanding that you missed, you might say, "I miss you. We don't seem to spend as much time together as we used to." If that doesn't seem to get things back on track, be prepared to let it go. Focus on the positive aspects of the friendship, the lessons you've learned, and move on.

Not every situation in life has to have a conclusion or a closure. Most closures are based on the negatives of a situation anyway, so if you miss out on that, who cares? Instead, focus on visualizing and opening yourself up to a friendship that will work better for you in the future. Dwelling on the anger you feel toward this person will only drag you down energetically and spiritually. Picture putting your anger into a box and burning it—*voilà!* You've released it; it's gone, and you won't carry that negative energy into a new friendship.

Unrequited Business Relationships

Marvin and Doug were a great team and accomplished more together as a team than anyone else in their company. Marvin loved the idea of being able to toss ideas around with someone who was on the same page, so to speak. They both benefited from their joint ventures, and Marvin would often comment that they could go far in the business with their two minds. Doug never said too much in response, but Marvin thought Doug was just being modest and serious and was not into talking much about their accomplishments and future projects.

Marvin would go home every evening bragging to the family about what a great duo they were and that they would probably both be promoted. His wife said she thought this guy sounded like "all business" and suggested that Doug might up and leave the company if he had the opportunity to go elsewhere. Marvin said Doug would never leave for another job, not when they were making a bundle together. But he did begin to think that perhaps his set-up with Doug wasn't as secure as he'd believed. He started to notice every little thing that might indicate that Doug was looking for another job. Marvin started to worry, and his anxiety grew worse every day.

Eventually, Doug did land a job with another company. He shook Marvin's hand, wished him well, and he was gone. Marvin was feeling angry and cheated at this point. He thought they were the dynamic duo waiting to conquer the world with their intellect and know-how. He became emotionally invested in the idea that finally he was a team player with someone, and that was even okay, until the prevailing emotion became anxiety over the possibility of Doug leaving. As time went on, Marvin focused on the negative, thus creating a negative situation.

Did Marvin's wife make Doug leave with her thoughts? Of course not, but she may have added fuel to the fire. If Doug had already been tossing the idea around, her added energy helped. She sent out the vibration "he will be leaving" then Marvin started to believe that Doug was leaving, and there we have the snowball effect. So, the minute the emotion got involved, it vaulted negativity out the office window and into the universe. The universe replied, "Okey dokey. You will get what most dominates your mind, which is Doug leaving."

How to prevent a similar situation from happening to you? Don't become so tangled up in someone else that you feel as though you couldn't go on without him as a business partner. Have belief in yourself; that creates a positive energy. Encourage the other person to be confident in his own abilities; that also creates a positive energy. Don't worry about what the other person is doing. Work together to build and to maintain a positively charged relationship, and chances are the partnership will go on and on.

Unrequited Love Affairs

The law of attraction states that you have to want something and put real emotion behind it to make it happen and then you must allow it to come into your life. So then why are there so many lonely people out there who were rejected by people they really loved? These jilted folks knew what they wanted—and talk about emotion, they were in love with the other person! (That sounds like plenty of sincere emotion to me.) Aren't you supposed to get what you want if you really feel it? Furthermore, these people were open to allowing love to come to them, so why didn't the law of attraction work in their relationships? Is it just not working in these cases?

Let me tell you a story about my friend, we'll call her May, who became involved with a man she worked with—we'll call him Brian. They flirted around the lunchroom for months and then one day as they were leaving for the day, he offered to help her fix the fence in her yard that she had been complaining about. Well, let's just say he fixed one gate and opened another. The relationship was *on*. For a while it centered around Brian coming by to fix things around May's house—always on weeknights, never during, say, a Sunday afternoon. The dates always ended by the light of the moon or at the crack of dawn the following morning. I'm sure you get the picture. There were never any dinner dates, excursions on the town, meeting of the families—nothing like that.

Despite this, May fell in love with him. She rationalized that they never went anywhere even for a quick sandwich because he was just too busy. She started planning their future in her mind. So she visualized, thought about what she wanted (him), and had the emotion behind it. Still, there was no commitment from Brian.

This went on for 3 years. During that time, May found out that he took other women out, but never her. She also learned that he had been married four times. This didn't deter her feelings—she started to believe that he was afraid of love or commitment out of fear it might not work.

Despite all of this, she thought that according to the law of attraction, she should end up with this guy. After all, she knew what she wanted, she had the emotion to back it, and she was willing to allow it. The hook is even though they were intimately compatible, to put it nicely, they were not resonating on the same energetic level as far as commitment goes. Brian had even told her that he was not a "relationship person!" So, right there, we know that his thoughts were not the same as hers.

Brian was 100 percent sure from the beginning that May was not "the one" (or in his case, the *next* one). She was sure that she loved him and wanted to be with him, but because all she received in return was … nothing (at least in the way of love), she doubted herself from time to time. His vibration was stronger than hers, and he's the one who got what he wanted from their relationship. I don't know that he was a believer in the law of attraction, but he certainly sent out a vibe to the universe that said, "I want a purely sexual relationship with May." He never wavered from that, and that's what he attracted.

Attracting Great Relationships

What can you learn from May's sad experience? When you want to find that special person, be specific and open—but *not* specific as to the person. You can't focus on forcing someone to love you, because that person has his or her own mind-set and his or her own wants, and those vibrations are every bit as strong as yours. Instead, think of the spirit or the specific type of person you want to find (kind, funny, tall, rich, smart, whatever you want). Focus on it, and that person will align with your vibration.

Here's an example of traits that someone who's looking for a romantic partner might ask for:

I am asking for …

- ◆ A partner who understands that I am in the medical field and my work will have to come first on occasion.

- ◆ Someone who is done having children.

- ◆ Someone who is taller than me because that makes me feel protected.

- ◆ Someone who loves horses.

- ◆ Someone who makes over $100,000 a year. (This is not shallow, if this is what you want. Go for it.)

- ◆ Someone who has the same spiritual or religious beliefs I do.

- ◆ Someone who is already emotionally mature, who I won't have to raise along with my children. (The universe has a sense of humor. It's all happy vibration that makes it work.)

Continue to make your list and write down anything you want that you know in your heart is realistic and that you really believe. The law of attraction says you can have anything, but you really have to *believe* in what you're asking for. So, if you want someone who is worth a billion dollars and can fly to the moon at will without any aircrafts, that's fine. But you have to ask yourself realistically if you really believe this particular person exists. If in your heart and soul you think he or she does, and if you can connect to the vibrational signal of your higher power, and if you think this is right, then fine. But if you have a doubt in your mind that it's perhaps not the most realistic scenario, then you are not on a vibrational signal for success.

Negative Friends?

"Make your friends before you need them" is something someone told me, and I never forgot it. When we are down, having a friend to lean on can do wonders. Of course, we aren't supposed to focus on negative things in life, but we are human, and most of us have not been programmed to live the law of attraction since childhood, so every once in a while, most of us find ourselves unable to face the world alone, so to speak. During these times, a friend is often the only salve for your wounded ego or heart. However, sometimes that friend can think she is helping you, but she's actually making things worse. You can avoid being caught in these situations if you know what to watch out for—and what to look for—in the best kinds of pals.

Feigned Support Affects Your Intentions

Some people are what I call yes men or women when it comes to being supportive. They appease you and agree with everything you say because they are afraid to tell you the truth. They think one thing, yet say another, like "Sure, I think your boyfriend is great!" when they're really thinking, "He is just about the biggest loser I've ever met." Or perhaps they say, "Oh, you're so lucky to have that job!" when they really think, "You're in *way* over your head."

Friends often do this sort of thing out of love, but they are doing more harm than good. First of all, they're thinking about your problems when you're not around, but offering you false praise or pointless advice when they're with you. Therefore, their suggestions or spoken opinions clash with the true vibrations they are sending out in regard to your well-being, leading to more chaos in your life! The best thing to do if you are in dire straits regarding a relationship, job, or any pressing matter is to ask your friends to wish you well and to focus on a positive future for you, instead of focusing on the things you're doing wrong.

When a friend asks for your opinion of a situation you disapprove of, be honest without being hurtful or negative. Phrase your response in terms of what's best for your friend, like, "I really think you deserve a boss who treats you better."

Like-Minded Friends Are Power Sources

"Like attracts like" is important in any level of relationship. It's interesting to have friends of all different philosophies, careers, and age groups, but when you find someone who has the same basic values, ideas, or upbringing, there is indeed a bond. It's comfortable knowing you don't have to explain yourself, because this person has also been there and done that.

Does that mean the best relationships are with people who are very similar to us on most levels? Yes and no. Friendships of any kind are usually based on like-mindedness. But it's the "Where are you going now?" aspect of the relationship that needs to be in sync for a relationship to continue. How many of us have left friends behind because they just refused to grow up and come into the adult world? (And by refusing to grow up, I'm talking about friends who are still into binge drinking, experimenting with all sorts of illicit drugs, and not working when they're in their 30s or 40s and beyond.) At that point, a common background doesn't mean nearly as much as a common, positive outlook for the future.

And that brings me to my last point: no matter what kind of relationship you're talking about, use the law of attraction to try to organize your life around people who are positive. These people are not jealous if you become successful. They support you in your endeavors. And they know that your positive outlook and happiness will result in an energetic vibe that will benefit them as well.

CHAPTER 14

Business, Social Media, and Technology

Social media can stimulate positive and negative emotions in us whether we use it recreationally, just to connect with old friends, or use it to promote ourselves with the intention of being successful on a business level. On the one hand, we can engage in fun conversations and groups that we might otherwise not have access to. On the other hand, we read things we don't agree with, we might get into arguments with complete strangers, and—especially for people who are using social media for business—if they get a thumbs down, discouraging comments, and dislikes, they can become disheartened. They may walk away from a project or endeavor all together.

Reacting to Social Media

The law of attraction does not give us power over people, but we do have power over how we react and whether we align vibrationally to what others say to or about us. It can be frustrating when people are bashing you when they really don't know who you are, what you feel, or your intention. Your opinion is not in sync with theirs.

Dealing with the Negative

When you are thriving or beginning to blossom, jealous people will try to bring you down. They want you to be like they are. You know who you are, and they simply don't. So, what are your options? Of course, you can forget social media altogether, but will you lose business because you are not marketing yourself on social media? Was that your ace in the hole?

You don't necessarily have to ban yourself from social media. Just do it differently. You need to be supported, not dispirited. Stop trying to please everyone—it simply can't be done. We all vibrate at different frequencies, and some people are just not a fit for each other. And if you are disheartened, you will create more disappointments as you focus on those sad thoughts. You will generate an atmosphere of failure around yourself.

Sometimes when you're using social media as a platform to sell something or promote yourself, it's best to get established in the "real world" first so you have confidence and a protective shield around you. Meaning, if you are already on the road to success, you most likely won't change your mind before you find success, as can be the case on social media. I've seen many people who gave up because they paid too much attention to negative feedback and just couldn't deal with it. This is a huge mistake.

For example: there was a woman named Karen who decided to open an online store and sell her swimsuit coverups. She designed them and sewed them herself. They were beautiful, and one size fit most. As she started to sell them and advertise them on social media, she found people complaining about pulled threads, not fitting right, delivery, etc. These things could have all been corrected. Instead of using those comments as constructive criticism, which would have improved her product in the long run, she got very depressed. Because of a few people who were downright mean, she gave in to the negativity, stopped production, and went back to working a regular job she did not like.

When you think pessimistic thoughts, it's bad enough. But when people put their rejection in writing in a place where others can see it, a snowball effect is developed—more negatives coming from everywhere. Karen gave in to the negative vibrational pull.

Promoting Confidence

If this happens, it's up to you to set the motion going positive again. Your inner self doesn't live in the past; it wants to go forward, and forward you must go. Start focusing again about aligning yourself with what you want to achieve. Some people don't realize what they actually do when they are critical and how the law of attraction is cumulative. The more people who are focused on you not doing well, the more it is likely to happen. One way to defend yourself is to forgive them and then set the issue aside. If you lie in bed at night thinking about how someone did you wrong or how they want to do you wrong, you are creating a vibrational match, which you don't want in this case.

If you find this happening, you should post something where you know you will get good feedback. Perhaps if Karen had said that she was updating her line and coming out with a new fabric, and everyone who purchased in the next few days was getting a free gift, it would have lifted her vibration. It would have made some of her followers think better of her and allowed her to start to recover emotionally and to see new potential. As I've repeated throughout the book: your emotions are what you have to pay attention to. The happier you are, the happier you will be.

Ditching the Undesirable

Another way to negate undesirable vibes is to remove yourself from looking at your social media for a while and maybe having someone else handle it for you.

You might say the platform will be down while changes are being made. In this case, you are stopping that snowball effect by removing yourself from it.

Be encouraging to those who are very supportive, by the way. Don't give just a thank you, go on a little about how much it meant to you to hear something you wanted to hear. Let's go back to Karen for an example. If someone commented that Karen made the best swimsuit coverups she ever bought, Karen should have been effusive in her thanks: "It means so much to receive a message like this! I work hard to deliver the best product possible. Which coverup did you choose? Can you post a picture?" The more you write back to positive people, the more it encourages them to write more. Again, the law of attraction at work—but this time on your side. (Of course, we know it doesn't take sides, it just gives you what you want!)

Social Media: It's Personal!

Technology is a product of expansion. The more people use it, love it, benefit from it, and get excited about it, the more it develops. We all know, whether we use it or not, that social media has become the way of socializing these days. It's the path of least resistance, and the easiest way to connect with people. Almost everyone has a Facebook or Twitter account. People meet all the time on Match.com, Bumble, and OkCupid. It's become an expectation that you have some sort of presence on social media, and this has opened a can of worms that simply can't be closed.

Your Online Presence

Online conversations tend to be a great example of lowered inhibitions without the use of illicit substances. That is to say that there are a lot of people out there who will say things online that they would never have the nerve to say to someone face to face. It's as though the keyboard gives some people instant courage to be confrontational, oppositional, or downright mean! None of us wants to be insecure, and yet, we are trained by our own programming to pass judgment on ourselves by the way others judge us—for better or worse! That's where social media can help or hurt. It vibrates both ways.

Social media can be lots of fun, informative, and a means to get to know people better. These are all good things. But there are those folks who are out to be hurtful. Don't feed into their vibration, or they will make you feel inferior, because when you are looking to others for approval, they are not necessarily connected to source energy like you are.

Dealing with Internet Trolls

An internet troll can make you feel woefully inferior. Remember that these are people who are not in touch with their highest selves, and likely aren't even aware of their innate ability to connect to a higher power. These are folks who like to stir the pot and enjoy upsetting people. It might be helpful to keep in mind that someone who enjoys hurting others most likely has deep psychic wounds that need healing. Having said that, sometimes on social media we have to kill hate with kindness. Don't be afraid to flatter people—without lying, of course. People enjoy being flattered, no matter what they may tell you. They will eventually start to tune in to your vibration. Just a tiny compliment can go a long way sometimes. Even if you haven't met someone in person, you might comment on how they write or their sense of humor.

Recourses for Negativity

Now let's say that someone writes a comment on one of your pictures: "You look like a buffalo in that dress." Shocking! Take a breath. Don't let them take your positive power. If you have to write back, tell them. "I like buffalo! LOL You are always so funny!" See what happened there? You didn't give in to the reaction this person wanted and then you took it a step further by saying something nice about them. Turning the tables like this will usually surprise someone, as they tried to hurt you and it didn't work. Hopefully they will think twice about their negativity, but even if they continue with their behavior, you haven't added to it. You've stopped this negative train in its tracks.

The alternative—feeding into the negativity—usually goes something like this:

♦ Someone makes a nasty comment.
♦ You respond with shock and scold this person for being nasty.

- ◆ This person responds with something even nastier.
- ◆ Other friends jump in; mean comments start flying and escalating, and you've got a big mess on your hands—or, more accurately, on your page.
- ◆ This carries over into real life, as it's all but impossible to set the weight of personal insults aside, especially after you've spent a significant amount of time reading mean comments and thinking about how to really zing this person.

It can be difficult to ignore someone who is constantly baiting you with negativity, and even more difficult when that person is a family member, a mutual friend of many other friends, or someone you do business with. Don't lose your entire network of friends or business contacts because of one bad social-media apple. If changing your reaction to them doesn't work, make sure you've checked in with your mind-set. Setting it to a positive vibration is protective and beneficial all the way around.

Here's a good example: I had a friend Dan, who was broke more often than not. His long-time real-world friends would post their huge successes online, bragging about new houses, boats, vacations, promotions—you name it. Dan, meanwhile, was happy with his subsistence-level income because it meant he could spend more time doing what he truly loved, which was fishing.

Some of his wealthy online friends would even make comments about how it was time for Dan to get a "real job" and question what he planned to do about retirement, as these people assumed he didn't have a penny set aside in savings. Even after reading these comments, Dan didn't harbor any negative feelings. In fact, he would always comment on other people's successes and tell them how happy he was for them. He told me that when he did this, he knew that positive vibrations were coming his way—and you know what? He was right! He is one of the happiest people I know, he always has enough money to get by, and he refuses to take negative comments personally.

Here's another recourse for negativity: if someone is being extraordinarily abusive on social media, just block them. Don't think twice about it or fret over it. Know that you can't fix every situation, and you can't pull every negative person into the positive sphere.

Remember, especially when you're on social media: you are not personally responsible for the spiritual development of everyone out there. Not even philosophers or gurus take on such a huge task! What you can do is introduce them to more positive ways by living those ways yourself. You are keeping your vibration high when you do this, and the universe will always respond in kind.

CHAPTER 15

Money, Jobs, and Careers

What if you could roll out of bed every morning and feel invigorated about the prospect of spending the day at work? Whatever it is that you desire—whether it's work that defines your life, or a job you can leave behind at the end of the day—you can find it using the law of attraction.

Some people, of course, will say, "If I can have anything I want by using the law of attraction, then why should I have to work at all? What if I want to lie around the house all day, every day?" Well, I'll also address these types of requests in this chapter. What you'll find, ultimately, is that anything you ask of the universe must feel right and realistic; otherwise, it's just a waste of time!

Finding the Right Line of Work

There's that old saying, "Find something you like to do and then figure out how to make money from it." I don't necessarily believe that everyone needs to make a lot of money in order to be happy, but I do believe that it's important to enjoy what you do. When you know in your heart that a particular line of work will make you happy, then you're free to ask, allow, and receive its benefits into your life.

But some people have a hard time getting to this first step. They can't seem to find any line of work that makes them feel satisfied. If you're one of these people, it may help for you to take a look at the things that produce negative energy in your current job and then decide whether you can use the law of attraction to help neutralize those annoyances. You might just find that you're already *in* the right line of work—you just had to learn to attract happiness!

Your Current or Most Recent Work Situation

Before you can define what kind of work or career you would like to have, take a minute to reflect on where you are now careerwise, and write down in your journal what you have learned from your experiences. Include the positives and the negatives.

Here's an example: My job has shown me that …

- I am not a people person and would be better working by myself, either in a stockroom or behind a computer.
- I like working in the evenings as opposed to the mornings.
- Working with people I like energizes me; working with people I don't care for drains me.
- I will never work for someone else again.

There is no right or wrong way to fill in your ideal job criteria. Be completely open and honest with yourself and write what you feel. Don't analyze it, and don't try to write what you think you *should* feel. You'll end up exactly where you started: confused, frustrated, and stuck in a rut.

As you read over your responses, remember that whatever you have been through on the job has been a learning experience. Have gratitude for those experiences, even if they weren't exactly happy moments. You've gained new insights into yourself, which will set you on the road to where you want to be.

Gratitude is an essential part of attracting goodness and happiness into your life. No matter how terrible an experience has been, acknowledge that it has contained a life lesson. Each experience has made you who you are today and who you will be tomorrow—and that's something to be grateful for!

Now I want you to reread the things you've listed about your current workplace and the lessons you've learned. It's good for each of us to narrow down our wants, so long as they're charged with positive energy. Is there anything on that list that's within your control to change by enlisting positive energy and a more positive viewpoint? If you were able to change one or two things, might you enjoy your current job more? I'll explain this idea more in the following section.

Bad Vibes in the Workplace

We've all had jobs where we felt downtrodden, oppressed, or generally useless. Guess what that kind of feeling does to the vibe you send out to the universe? Nothing good. It doesn't help to dig you out of the rut you're in; it only serves to dig you in deeper.

If you spend all day at work thinking about the reasons you don't like your job, focusing on your dislike of your coworkers, wishing you could sleep in a little later, hoping that everyone around you would disappear so you can work in peace and quiet, can you really expect things to get any better? No way! That negative energy is a magnet for *more* negative energy.

When you focus negative energy on another person, you may actually be helping his or her cause. Whenever the universe receives a boost of energy surrounding a particular person, it sends *back* a boost of energy. Your thoughts about your irritating coworker might be feeding his success!

Let's say you've always been good with numbers and you find yourself working in an accounting office. It's a job you should theoretically enjoy, but you can't stand your cubical mate. He's a real schmoozer, a trait you despise. You also believe he's earning more than you are because he just bought a flashy new car and he's always happy, happy, happy. You just know that you'd be happy, too, if you were earning what he's making.

Can you see how this situation is plagued by negative energy? How might you change things? Well, for starters, I'd recommend taking your focus off your coworker in the next cubicle and putting it on yourself. Think about what you want to achieve and then go after it. There's no reason in the world that you can't be as happy and successful as this guy—it's just a matter of where your intent is.

Once you take your focus off despising your coworker and place it on your own desires, I'm betting you'll find a new kind of peace and tranquility in the workplace. Maybe it's still not the perfect job for you, but it will be easier for you to have some gratitude for this experience and take that along with you into your next job.

Advancing Your Career

At some point, most of us want to advance in our line of work, whether that means landing a job promotion or finally getting the part that will put your acting career on the fast track. Part of moving forward in a career field is acknowledging that new doors will be opening up. If you don't truly want what's behind those doors, the universe will feel that vibe and answer in kind.

An actress I know auditioned for a role in a Broadway musical. She had the kind of talent most people only dream of, and she seemed like a shoo-in for the part (or at least as much of a shoo-in as anyone can be on Broadway). Well, the part went to someone else, much to everyone's surprise. She packed her bags and left New York for good. After she had settled in California, she told me she realized she had sabotaged her audition by putting most of her energy into thinking about moving to Hollywood. The musical would have been a stepping-stone on her way to her ultimate destination: a film career. So, even though she prepared herself well for her Broadway audition, her energy was already focused elsewhere. When she didn't get the part, she realized that she needed to be where her energy and her intention already were.

So, what does this mean to those of you working in cubicles? Before you set your eyes and energy on some ultimate prize of a job, make sure it's what *you* truly want. Fighting the universe to secure a position that goes against your true desires (or even your true nature) is a losing battle.

What I Want to Be ...

How do you know which career paths work with your true nature? Break down your desires. Here are some examples: I would like a job or career that would ...

♦ Allow me to travel.

♦ Put me in the public eye.

♦ Gross six figures from working at home.

♦ Enable me to meet interesting people but still maintain a low-key lifestyle.

♦ Let me work in shorts and a T-shirt.

Mention children, pets, the ballet, and anything you like that you have a passion for, whether it's eating doughnuts or planting flowers. Consider working inside or outside, in a big city or a small village. Be as specific as you can. Through this exercise, your thoughts should be beginning to take shape and bring a bit more clarity to your goals. Paula Poundstone, a comedian and author said humorously, "Adults are always asking little kids what they want to be when they grow up because they're looking for ideas."

Even though her quote is comical, she had a point. Children are looking for things they like and are fun. We should do that, too.

At this point, if you cannot conclude what you want to do, you should at least have figured out what you *like*. At a bare minimum, you are narrowing down the field. Don't be afraid to write down something even if you think it is nearly impossible. The important thing about narrowing down your perfect job is that you are sincere and take this seriously. Asking the universe to make you ruler of the world isn't going to feel right to you, and thus can never come to be.

I assure you, by the time you're finished reading this book, you'll *know* it's within the realm of reality!

A Day in the Life

Write in your journal about a perfect day in your work or career. It might read something like, "I see myself in a tall office building with a view of the mountains. I am dressed like an executive and I'm busy, but I'm happy. I have a secretary and fashion pictures all around me, but I'm not sure of my position."

Add this page to your journal and complete the sentence: My perfect day on the job would be ...

Now take a minute and consider how it makes you feel when you think about your dream job—but run through a typical day in your mind. You might be surprised to discover that the "perfect" job makes you squirm! Here is an example from a friend of mine who thought she wanted to be a massage therapist. Kirsten writes,

> When I thought about my idea of being a massage therapist, at first it felt good. But then I remembered speaking to a massage therapist who said that she had had to quit because her hands hurt. Even so, I still think it's a good idea for me, at least for now. But I don't think massage therapists make much money and I need cash now.
>
> So many people are becoming message therapists, I might have to fight for clients. Suddenly, I don't feel encouraged about this choice, but I suppose I am looking at the negatives and not the positives, such as having my own business. Then again, I don't have the money to rent a space and maybe it would be better to work for someone else. But then I would have to split my earnings and follow someone else's schedule.
>
> Ugh, and what if I don't have a window in the room and all the clients are sweaty? That doesn't sound like fun. No, the more I think about this, it just doesn't make me feel good at all. It makes me feel like my bank account is already depleted from paying rent, my hands already hurt, and I'm gagging for air from the weightlifter who didn't bother to take a shower after the gym. Get me out of here!

Suffice it to say, Kirsten gave up on the massage-therapy idea fairly quickly. She also loved all kinds of music, so her next idea was to find work in a music store. I asked her how that made her feel. (Remember in Chapter 5, we talked about investing positive emotions into requests.) She said, "Well, I was raised in a musical family. I love everything from rap to classical, and my sound equipment must be worth more than my convertible. But I really want a job where I can help people. Plus, I don't want to tell my friends and family that I work in a music store—I'm not a college kid, I'm 48! What am I going to do, work for a 20-year-old boss?"

Keep in mind, it's okay to have positive and negative thoughts about your ideal line of work. However, whenever possible, try to take negative vibes and rework them to the positive side. For example, instead of saying, "I don't want to work for anyone else," say, "I want to be my own boss." It's just better to work with positive energy!

As you can see, Kirsten had definite ideas about her perfect job, even though she hadn't yet defined what that job would be. And I was starting to see a pattern here. She did not want to manage her own business or anyone else's, but her passion was really for healing and music. I suggested she focus on a career involving music and healing using the law of attraction. It was not a super-specific request, but it was enough for her to start attracting what she wanted. She focused her intent on this request each evening and tried to envision how her perfect job would make her feel.

About 3 months later, Kirsten met a man who is a physical therapist. They got to talking about health, and Kirsten mentioned that she believed music was a powerful force for healing. Well, the man was so interested in what she had to say, he invited her to come to a session and play music for one of his clients. One thing led to another, and after studying in an approved program, she has become a music therapist. (A job that entails using talk therapy in conjunction with music—inspiring, soothing, or uplifting … the type of music depends on the needs of the individual person—to heal clients' emotional wounds.) No touching people, no management, and all the healing she can give!

Lessons Learned

Kirsten had such a passion for music therapy that she basically created a career by sending flyers to hospitals and private medical practitioners, not to mention seminar events on healing through music. Because the joy was there, she found her niche.

So, exactly what did Kirsten do to attract the career she loves?

- She defined what she liked, which was music and healing.

- When she thought about the two separate entities, she felt good about both, but she had no idea how she would combine the two of them.

- She kept visualizing herself being happy when she came home at the end of the day from a career she loved. She thought more about how she wanted to *feel* rather than which specific career would deliver her peace of mind.

What's the best lesson to learn from Kirsten? The initial work wasn't easy, but many worthwhile things aren't simple. When her eyes were opened to the possibility of becoming a certified music therapist, she immediately believed that it was possible. Part of the reason this was so easy for her is because she took the time to weed out what she wanted from what she didn't want. She focused on her desire, believed it could happen, and allowed it to enter her life!

Tips to Stay on Track

The law of attraction isn't like a fast-food drive-through. You don't simply say, "I want this, this, and this," and have it hand-delivered to you in 3 minutes flat. You have to be patient and let the universe work everything out. To help stay focused on your goal, keep track of the things you're doing to send out those positive vibes. For example, if you're interested in working aboard a cruise ship, you might write the following in your journal:

- **Day One:** Today I got the phone number and email address of the cruise-line recruiter to inquire about applying for a position.

- **Day Two:** I called the cruise line and talked to Mary Smith, the human resources director, about the qualifications I will need for various positions.

- **Day Three:** I visualized myself working on a cruise line, from the beginning of a workday to the end. The idea excites me!

- **Day Four:** I focused on the picture of the cruise line that I keep on my bulletin board. I really think I would feel at home on a ship.

There is no set time period to take action on your goal. Set a time frame that is comfortable for you. Try to have some type of set schedule where you focus on your desires, like every morning or every other day. Sometimes lying in bed in the morning works well, as you are still in an altered state of consciousness (a meditative mode), and it enables you to visualize more readily. Experiment with what works.

Upon getting out of bed or moving on from wherever ever you decided to focus, don't forget to use pictures or drawings as a way to help you visualize. (You can read more about this in Chapter 6.) You're creating an air of expectation, which boosts your positive energy and puts your request right into the universe's ear, so to speak!

Upping Your Standard of Living

Is it alright to skip the whole line of work request and simply ask the universe to send some good old extra cash into your life?

There's nothing wrong with wanting material things or having a good life. We don't have to be poor to be good people. So, go ahead and ask to get on the gravy train—just make sure that you can believe in it and allow it into your life.

I've Got the Money, Honey

The law of attraction works by focusing on what you want, not what you lack. So, don't think "I don't have any money and I wish I had more." Instead think "I am going to attract extra capital into my life … after all, there is plenty for everyone."

For fun, let's attract $50. Why only $50? Because you are trying to reprogram yourself. The law of attraction knows no difference between $50 and $5,000,000, but *you do*, and because you will probably doubt that you can attract that kind of dough, the universe will sense your hesitation. Five million dollars won't feel like a realistic goal to you—at least at first—so you will negate the process before you even begin.

Take out a piece of paper and write $50 on it. Next to it, write down a date 10 days from the present date. As you do this, think that by some unusual means (in other words, not via your paycheck, but perhaps in a gift certificate or some sort of credit), you'll attract an additional $50 into your life. Put the paper in your wallet.

Three times a day or more, take a peek at that paper and think about how you will feel if you get that $50. Will you feel joyous because if it worked with $50, it could work with more? Or will you feel agitated that you didn't seek more to begin with?

Here are a few other ideas:

♦ Take a deposit slip from your checkbook and write $50 in the cash or check area and set it on your desk or dresser. Look at it daily.

♦ Every morning wake up and say, "That extra $50 is coming my way!"

♦ Find something you want to buy for $50 and think about it often, draw it, or cut it out of a magazine. Print it off a website on your computer. Just know you will have the extra money for the purchase.

We will talk more about visualization in the next chapter. But for now, this is a simple method that is very successful.

One last thing: remain positive. You don't want to attract money from a bank robber who throws the money in the back of your pick-up while fleeing the police. Focus your thoughts on attracting that $50 from a source that is legitimate.

Remember, if you think you are going to start to feel you are doing a lot of emotional work for a meager $50, then you won't attract the money due to your negative thoughts. But if you feel it's possible and realistic, use a small amount as an experiment. If you really, truly believe that you can attract a large amount of money from the get-go, then go ahead and ask for it. However, sometimes you have to take small steps rather than a big jump as you have not yet experienced what the law of attraction can do.

You really have nothing to lose by giving the law of attraction a chance. Focusing your energy on happiness and prosperity—instead of on what you lack—will bring you what you desire and deserve. Learn to let go of the negative thoughts about your job or financial situation, and see yourself in a future filled with success of every kind!

CHAPTER 16

Super-Focusing Your Requests

So, you think you understand the law of attraction? In fact, it may already be working well in your life. Now you're going to take things a step further by literally investing in your dreams and spending a little cash that you may have stashed away.

"What?" you may say. "Spend money on something that I don't even have yet?" Yep. By making actual strides toward your goals, you're telling the universe that you fully expect success. The universe says, "Well, all right, then you should have what you want." Some of the things I talk about in this chapter are major investments; most, though, are quick and easy (and cheap!). Your focus is what's most important. Can you believe and allow the law of attraction to work for you?

Buy It Now

You don't have to break the bank, as they say, to buy a few things that give you the feeling you are already on your way to your goal. By bringing just a few material reminders into your life now, you'll reinforce the feeling that everything is going along as it should be and it's only a matter of time before your desires come to fruition.

An Outfit Before the Date

Okay, you don't have a date planned, and you haven't had one in 3 years. You have put the law of attraction to work to find a mate. (We talked about this in Chapter 13.) It's time to buy a new outfit. Start your potential date off with something new, so that you don't have any old energy attached to your clothing.

You know the pieces of apparel you think work well for you, but put them on the back burner for a while. They might include your lucky shirt, that blouse that always draws attention, the cowboy boots that have that leather smell, giving them sex appeal, to name a few.

Don't get rid of these items; just don't use them to start your *new* dating life. These items have your old energy attached to them. It's not like a tag hanging off the side of your pants, but it's very real, and it affects the way you feel and the way you behave. (And if you haven't had a successful relationship in many, many years, then it's time to start thinking about how your behavior affects your energy and vice-versa.)

Romantic attachments aren't the only energy you should be concerned about when dressing for a date, though. Some articles of clothing may carry negative vibes from a certain time in your life. Let's say you have a gorgeous jacket that you love to wear, but you purchased it right around the time you were fired from your first job. Even if you wear that jacket so often that you think it has no specific ties to that period of time, those links still exist. The anger, the insecurity, the upheaval of that time is attached to that jacket. So, save it for a relatively unimportant event—a trip to the theater, for example, or a lunch date with your sister—but *don't* wear it on a date!

Even if the outfit you were wearing when your ex proposed is something you've worn on other occasions, even if you had that outfit long before you met him or her, even if you receive numerous compliments when wearing it, buy something new and do it now. The mere fact that you can simply look at an outfit and associate it with an old romantic attachment is enough to doom your dating future (at least as long as you're trying to woo someone new while wearing it). Pack it away and try a new look for a new mate.

Gourmet Pots Before the New Kitchen

Because they're so darn expensive to redesign or build from scratch, a new kitchen is sometimes only a dream or a wish. If you are trying to attract a new kitchen and you have asked, believed, and are now in allowing or receiving mode, you may as well look for a few kitchen items you can buy now.

This is not frivolous at all. You need pots to cook food. Food keeps us alive. So, new gourmet pots, new dishes, and so on are all part of your dream. You may not need all of them, but there must be something new for the kitchen you've had your eye on.

Make at least one small purchase and pack it away in a special place or box, and write on the box "new kitchen." Visualize how that plate or vase will look on your new counter. Is there a batch of fresh-baked cookies on that plate? Are there flowers from your garden in the vase? How do you feel when you see them in your new kitchen? Use that positive feeling to focus on your belief and allowing.

An iPhone Case Before You Have the iPhone

Not all people, but the majority, want the latest technology. If you can't afford the latest version of the iPhone or the cell phone you want, get the accessories instead. Install your cell phone holder in your car before you get the product. Better yet, get it before you get the car!

Every day when you look at it think "It will be there soon." And then *believe* it.

Always keep your focus on what you want, not what you're lacking. Positive energy reinforces your request and helps to bring it to fruition.

Skinny Pants Before the Weight Loss

You're a size 16 and you're hoping to slim down to a size 12. Or you're a size 10 and looking to get down to a 6. Go ahead and buy those skinny pants—you know, the ones without elastic that you're afraid to wash in fear they may shrink. Get the style and color you want. Once you lose the weight, your favorite store may not have the look you love so much now!

Hang those pants in your closet so they are the first thing you see when you enter; or fold them and put them on your dresser, well in view; or hang them on a hook where you look at them every day. They're a visualization tool. Close your eyes and think: How will losing weight affect my health? My mood? My opinion of others? Can you *feel* those changes? Can you direct that positive energy into the universe as you ask for a slimmer figure?

I Still Don't Buy It

If you don't see how buying something small can help you get something big, you aren't believing very much.

The buying bit is sending out a vibration that says, "I already have what I desire, so I need this other item to go with it." The universe responds, "You already have the accessories? Oh my, I better send that big item out fast before you notice you don't have it."

But don't just take my word for it, *try* it. Believe it. And then enjoy the benefits.

Take Action

Bear in mind, you can't lead from behind. Making a small purchase as a visual reminder is one thing, but now try really moving your body and mind toward your goals. Physical action really gets your intent cooking. You're doing something, you're focusing on why you're doing it, and it's easier to think that your desire will soon be a reality. This goes a long way toward boosting belief, which in turn goes a long way toward boosting your intent, and this positive cycle just feeds itself.

Pack Before Your House Sells

If your house is for sale, go searching for those free boxes to pack your household items in. Start by packing small things and items you rarely use to get yourself ahead of the process. In this process, you boost your belief vibe and your house sells quickly.

Here's a good example of what I'm talking about. Jim and Leslie had a beautiful home in Hawaii. The cost of living there was too much for their modest incomes, and they decided to sell their home and move inland. As the real-estate market was not booming and their house was very pricey, the realtor told them it could take over a year to sell the property for fair market value.

They decided not to pay attention to this negative report and to treat the house sale as though it had already taken place. They gathered boxes and packing supplies and packed up dishes and other items they knew they would not use. They packed most of their clothing and only left enough out to get them by for a few weeks.

Everyone thought they were being unrealistic and would shake their heads and say things like, "That poor couple! They're packing up, but they will never sell that house!" However, Jim and Leslie persisted and did not allow the negative thoughts and attitudes of others to shake their belief that the house would sell.

When the packing process was complete, Jim and Leslie just relaxed and waited. In the meantime, they were cruising down a street in a nearby neighborhood and saw a beautiful house for sale. They discovered the mortgage on the potential new house would be half the cost of their current house.

Then they broke the rule of all real-estate rules and bought a new home before selling their old house. They were to move in 2 months. If their present house didn't sell in that time, they would have to carry two mortgages, and they could not afford that at all. Again, friends called them irresponsible, illogical, and flighty. When people start to discourage you in the pursuit of your dreams, simply change the subject. Or tell them thanks, but you want to remain positive.

Jim and Leslie also bought furniture for their new house. Leslie bought a "for sale" sign and put it in their living room. Using a large black marker, she wrote "sold" across the sign. They looked at it every day. (You really couldn't miss it in the middle of the living room.) One week before the closing on the new house, they got a call from their realtor. He had potential buyers who wanted to view their home. It was love at first sight, and the sale closed 30 days later.

Am I encouraging you to buy another house before you sell yours? No. But I am encouraging you to believe in your goal and do what you feel will work. It's all vibration. Packing, buying another house, and so forth was putting out the vibration that their house was close to selling.

Most people said Jim and Leslie were just lucky and should never have taken that chance. Others said that if they tried it again, it would never work. Regardless of all the negative reactions, Jim and Leslie say they would do it again. They kept their eyes on the prize and just knew that everything would work out.

Celebrate Your New Achievement

What would your friends do if you told them to come over to your home to celebrate something, but kept the celebratory event a secret? They would probably show up with champagne and congratulations cards in pink and blue envelopes. They would enter your home where balloons and a big cake are the focus of the dining area. There you are all dressed up in your best attire, sporting a big smile and glowing.

They would be happy for you, no doubt about it. Then comes the question: "Well, why are we here today?" As you begin to speak, they would all draw near and put their glasses down in anticipation of a hand-clapping frenzy, and you say: "We are celebrating my future promotion!"

Future? They would assume you already got this new position but aren't starting for a month or two. No, you tell them, you are just anticipating it will happen. Why wait to celebrate?

The crowd would be scratching their heads and giving you lots of funny looks. Of course, there might be one or two who would cheer you on and say this party is a great idea. If you have sincere friends who really wish you well and can get into the celebration-before-the-goal mode, you'll be able to create a vibration that will be contagious. By the end of the night they would all start feeling that you have indeed secured that promotion. (We are counting on energy to heighten their mood and not an overabundance of champagne!)

Whenever you celebrate anything in the present or something that will take place in the future, and it brings you cheerfulness, you are creating more cheerfulness for the very thing you will be achieving. Remember, like attracts like. One celebration focused on future successes certainly has the potential to attract another.

Build a Two-Sink Bathroom When You're Single

If you go into a new house and see one sink in the master bedroom, it tells you one of a few things:

- The owner is cheap and won't spring for a second sink.
- The builder made a mistake.
- There is another master bathroom on the other side of the bedroom.
- The person is single and intends on staying that way.

What do a single sink and the law of attraction have in common? They have a lot in common if you are building a new home. This tells us where your mind-set is. If you want a relationship, think duo.

Have fun with the "duo" principle in all sorts of ways while you're waiting for your mate to come along. Buy a king-size bed. Clear out one side of your walk-in closet. Empty a dresser drawer. Make room for him or her!

These things should be making you smile, if not laugh, and that's the vibration you want to put out to source energy. You want to have positive, fun, cheery emotion behind everything you do. That way, you will attain your goal faster.

See It and Make It Happen

I've talked about visualization briefly in this chapter, but here are some specific methods that really work. I'm covering what seem to be the most popular issues here, but you can obviously personalize this process by changing the focus of your mental picture. In that case, just use the following as examples.

Picture a Slimmer You

Here are some quick ways to see yourself thinner with the minivisualization technique. Try a few of these methods at least three times a day. It doesn't matter if you repeat the same one or pick a new one each time—just give it a shot:

- Before you get on the scale, take a few seconds to look at the wall in front of you and visualize your ideal weight as it would look on your particular scale. (In other words, see the number itself, whether it's 120, 150, or 180.)

- Daily glimpses of that scale can make a bad situation worse, making you think, "I'll never lose this weight!" That, of course, sends a pretty strong message to the universe and guess what happens? Try weighing yourself just a couple of times a week and stay positive, no matter what the numbers say!

- If you are waiting for someone and watching the passers-by, imagine yourself walking where they are walking in the size and shape you are trying to attract.

- Use your cell phone and take a "before" picture of yourself, and don't let anyone see it. Know that in a few weeks or months, the "after" picture will be spectacular. What will you be wearing in the after picture; what will your hair look like, and where will you take the picture?

- Print out a picture from the internet, or cut out a picture from a magazine of someone who looks similar to you at the weight you want to attain. The picture does not have to be of a movie star but could be a mother-type model advertising a milk product or a guy cutting the grass. Post it on your refrigerator or put it anywhere you will look every day. Soon you will be replacing it with your own picture.

♦ Text or email a friend you haven't seen for years and tell him or her how you are really kicking off the pounds and how you did it. Then, instead of sending it, save the message until it comes true. It just feels good to write it, yes?

♦ Think about what you are going to do with your big clothes after you lose weight. Who will you give them to? Do give them to someone, if not to charity. Make a choice and see yourself dropping them off.

Above all, have compassion for yourself in your visualization. (Go back to Chapter 7 if you need a refresher on compassion.) Don't go down the self-pity road or the universe will see to it that nothing changes. Attracting weight loss is really only a thought (or two) away.

That said, before you can lose weight or fight any habit or addiction, you have to be in alignment with source energy. To do that, you have to feel the emotion that uplifts you to a place of happiness.

The number on the scale may not uplift you, but knowing you will be wearing those new clothes, saving money, or not smoking (etc.) should start you on your ascent. Think in terms of raising your vibration. Just be as clear as you can with your concentration or imagining.

See Your Perfect Mate

Make a list of what it is you want in a mate. Be as specific as possible and think about things like ...

♦ Age.

♦ Hair and eye color.

♦ Height and weight.

♦ Personality type.

♦ Sense of humor or intellect.

When I visualized my husband, I was not concerned about hair color. It didn't seem important. Because the law of attraction can work by default, I let it do its own thing. So, in my asking mode, I thought "Hair? That doesn't matter." Guess what? My husband doesn't have any! (Well, just a little around the edges!)

Quickie visualization routines used throughout the day and consistently are excellent ways to attract what you want in your life. Plus, they're a great diversion from your daily life. They provide you with the sense that you are doing something to help create what you want.

CHAPTER 17

Attracting Good Things to the Planet

Thus far, I've talked about health, happiness, prosperity, and spirituality—all things that will make us happy as individuals. But what about the planet that supports our bodies and souls so we can enjoy these things? Can we ask anything of the universe for this earth that we walk on? And if so, what would that be?

Well for one thing, we might concentrate our efforts on improving our collective consciousness. If we become more aware of Earth and its needs as a people, then Earth will reap the benefits.

"We Are the Ones We Have Been Waiting For"

The elders of the Hopi Nation, Oraibi, Arizona, tell us, "We are the ones we've been waiting for." This is so true. It seems we tend to think that the next generation, our children or grandchildren, will be the ones to make a difference. It reminds me of those signs you see that say, "Free beer tomorrow." Will you really hold out till then? What if tomorrow never comes?

Other new age theories hold that we are at the pinnacle of change. Earth is crying out for attention in the form of global warming and dissipating species; furthermore, the theories state that the generation of children being born onto the planet now are hyperaware of what needs to be done to save it. There's a built-in energy with these kids that you can almost feel (if you're around them enough, that is).

If these ideas and theories are correct, then Earth's energetic level is due for a big shift—and what happens then will be anybody's guess, but I have a feeling it's going to be for the best!

Never Too Late to Undo the Negative

We have all seen or heard that our planet is in need of attention and we are depleting its resources. Many people are taking action to preserve and protect the environment, such as "going green." Some of us are trying on a large scale and others are doing smaller things, like conserving energy in their homes and so on.

Any contribution is helpful. The law of attraction tells us like attracts like, and the more we focus on something, the more we get of it. So, if we focus on a healthy planet, we attract others into our lives who feel the same way.

When a train of thought is looked at more positively, the negative will be overpowered, so to speak, by the better attitude.

When all of these great minds sharing like energy get together, you may find yourself forming groups that go on to make a difference—and don't forget that there are lots of ways to get involved and make a difference, whether it's by being hands-on, literally cleaning up the rivers and forests, or by sending out emails that help the cause. The important thing is to be on the future peace train, not the past train wreck. Comments like "I can't believe what's happening to our polar bears!" do not help; they draw attention to the problem, to be sure, but they don't offer anything but negative energy. Comments like "We have great ideas for protecting the polar bears!" are better—they have a positive force for change behind them.

If you want to contribute to bettering the planet but don't want to get involved with any formal group, have a do-it-yourself healthy planet plan. Here are a few ideas:

- Visualize the things you don't like about the planet and see them getting better and better.
- Every day, imagine you hear or see something good on the news or internet about the planet's well-being.
- Buy a sign or make one that says "peace" and look at it periodically, thinking that one day it will be a reality.

This is your planet, your life; how could you not want to attract its health and the healthy attitude of love for all? The law of attraction is great for bringing great things into your personal life, but it's not all about having a new car. (Then again, you could visualize yourself driving around in an energy-efficient new vehicle as you travel a planet that is in harmony with all living things.) Show your gratitude for the universe and its grand design by caring for Earth.

Obsessive Preparedness for Negative Acts of Nature: Helpful or Harmful?

I live in Florida. When Hurricane Charley hit in 2004, we were the only house in the area left with electricity. We invited neighbors over for water, showers, and whatever we could do to help. Now, were we in some type of glitchy area and just by chance had power, or was there something more at work? Who knows? I like to think it was the law of attraction at its best.

I remember visualizing the hurricane passing all of us by, not just our individual house. And to some extent it did—our neighborhood had minimal power outages and only a few wind issues. Regardless, I have to wonder what would have happened if everyone in Florida would have seen the hurricane passing (back out to sea, not into another town) in their minds' eyes.

As the years passed after the hurricane, I had to wonder if there wasn't an overkill of hurricane products in the stores. Is this extreme focus on hurricanes attracting *more* hurricanes, I wondered? Is it irresponsible to buy hurricane shutters (because you feel that buying them means you're expecting it to happen, thus bringing it closer)?

Same goes for preparing for tornadoes, storms, and other acts of nature. There's nothing wrong with being prepared, but we don't need to dwell on the fear. We don't need to have special news shows at the beginning of hurricane season— before the first storm has even formed—to discuss what we're going to name each of the storms and what we'll do when we run out of letters. The minute there's a storm in the Atlantic, we don't have to think the worst and clutch our storm candles until they melt. That said, always act responsibly in any emergency. Take the safety first approach and then, when the work is done, concentrate on staying safe and free of danger or injury.

I like to think of buying emergency gear as things I can use for camping, and, hey, if there is an incident of nature that calls for these items, they will work for that as well. Admittedly, camping to me is a hotel without room service, but I still think it's better for me to believe I might go camping and to have those supplies on hand than to say to myself, "I need to know where these things are at all times just in case a tropical depression blows in today."

Attracting Peace

In Chapter 18, I'll talk about helping others and whether or not groups can attract things like world peace. The answer actually tends to be no—and not because the universe will only hear single-minded appeals. It's because every mind has a different history and its own perspective. When we try to send out a strong vibe as a group, all of those different perspectives can be contradictory, confusing, and not nearly as powerful as we'd hoped (or at least not powerful in the way we'd hoped they would be).

So, what can we, as individuals, do to help move the peace process along? Part of this includes shifting the population to embrace a new attitude and energy, something that's a long-term process but well worth the effort.

Should We Stop Watching the News?

As I write this book, there is conflict in many countries and our brave men and women are fighting or on watch to keep our country safe. People are polarized in their political beliefs, and the planet is being depleted of resources.

When you watch news reports about discrimination and injustice, do you find yourself enraged or do you focus and send your positive energy to the victims of such cruelty?

Every day, I hear people in casual conversation say things like this: times are bad; it's that politician's fault; the use of plastic will be our demise; fuel emissions are the problem; air pollution is the worst; water contamination is killing the fish; and the list goes on. Oh, my, my.

I want to shake those people and say, "So, say something good!" In fact, if I am in a grocery store line and hear such talk, I will very sweetly say something positive like, "It's a beautiful day today. I love this time of year!" People might look at me strangely and even leave the line. But every once in a while, I feel as though I've gotten through to someone and given them something positive to focus on. In improving one's mood even a tiny bit, people may remember that life holds many possibilities—and many of those possibilities are wonderful! So, even if there have been better days, remind yourself that it's only a matter of time before it turns around again.

As a population, we all need to learn to focus more on the positive possibilities and outcomes because our collective consciousness is what brings hopes or fears to fruition.

What If They Gave a War and Nobody Came?

There is an old Vietnam-era movie made in 1970 called *Suppose They Gave a War and Nobody Came.* It was actually a cute comedy about how an army base had a feud with the citizens of a nearby town. But I always loved the title and often wondered what would happen if *both* sides of a war had no recruits. Would the world leaders be forced to fight their own battles?

Well, you may be surprised to learn that the leaders, while they're certainly responsible for their own actions in voting for and waging aggression, are really fed by the energy of the people around them—the citizens who support them *and* the citizens who oppose them. Remember back in Chapter 6 when I told you that in order for any vibration to manifest itself, it has to have your focus? And remember when I said that focusing on negative thoughts only helps to bring them into reality? The universe receives strong vibrations of a positive or negative nature and then sends them back to us full force.

You need only look at any example of past war and conflict to see examples of negative or positive vibes taking hold. In World War II, for example, Americans who were not fighting on the front lines did their best to keep the home fires burning, so to speak. During the Vietnam era, young people from around the country flocked to Woodstock to support the peace effort. During more recent conflicts, however, we seem to be more divided than ever, which in turn seems to be leading us into more dicey situations both at home and around the globe.

Am I suggesting we ignore our leaders and let them run amok? No. I'm suggesting that we learn to focus on positive, peaceful resolutions and actions. When we, as a group of citizens, can learn to make optimism and constructive thought the center of our collective attention, then we will see a shift in energy. As the old saying goes, support what you love rather than opposing what you hate. It sounds like splitting hairs, but the shift of focus from negative to positive can literally change the world around you.

How to Hold a Peace Rally

My friend Susan Dobra, a teacher, writer, and peace activist, has been going to peace rallies since the 1960s. She says one thing she's learned over the years is that the best peace rallies are creative and fun and ... well, peaceful. Here's what she told me about how to use the law of attraction to plan a peace rally:

> Peace will only come through compassion and open-heartedness and forgiveness. It might feel good to stir up a crowd by whipping up some anger and righteous indignation aimed at the president or other leaders, the ones who keep making the same mistake of using wars and violence to solve problems. And there might even be a place for expressing anger, for people who need to work those feelings out.
>
> But the wisest among us know you can't fight fire with fire. You only escalate the damage that way. In the same way, you can't fight for peace. Anger, ultimately, won't get you there. If you want peace, you must *be* peace.
>
> So, when you're planning a peace rally, keep in mind that you want to affirm the value of being at peace. Start with a meditation or a silent circle to remember the dead. Take a moment from time to time throughout the event to hold a space for breathing and feeling compassion for those who are caught up in war and opposition. And even though there may be some firebrands who want to create a frenzy of emotion and energy at the rally, be sure to plan on bringing the energy back down at the end with a candlelight vigil or procession or prayer.
>
> One of my friends once saw me coming back from a peace rally with my favorite sign, which is simply a round picture of Earth with a peace dove superimposed. He called out to me, "What are you protesting?" "I'm not," I replied, "I'm advocating."
>
> At a true peace rally, we advocate for peace. We attract it to us by bringing it through us.
>
> One of the things I like to tell is a story about Mother Teresa, who reportedly was asked about her seeming lack of political activism. She said, "I was once asked why I don't participate in antiwar demonstrations. I said that I will never do that, but as soon as you have a pro-peace rally, I'll be there."

These days, social media gives everyone a platform, and too often, the platform is based on bashing a person in power. Thousands of followers jump on a bandwagon to add to the hate. What if we decided, instead, to send love and light to our leaders? If we believe in the idea of energy, then isn't it possible that sending messages of hate only makes a leader more determined to carry out acts of aggression or war? Prayers and meditation get bashed these days as being ineffectual and trite, but there has to be a reason why these methods of conveying love have lasted for millennia. If we really want others to follow a peaceful path, we have to lead by example.

So, there you have it: peace, love, and understanding (or compassion) are the keys to turning this planet around.

A Healthier Environment

I would love to walk into any place on Earth and not be concerned about food, water, radiation, and so on. How many of you are reading this and thinking, "Who wouldn't? But that probably will never happen."

The reality is that even though I would love for this to be the truth, I, too, doubt it because so much has already been programmed through default thinking. The good news is I think we could change it subtly, so things become better and better. And in the future, this could in fact be a possibility. So, teach your children well. As you learn to attract good things, trying to make positive changes in the here and now, remind them that the cycle should never stop.

"That Will Make You Sick!" but Only If You Say So

Don't eat that! This is fattening! This raises your cholesterol! That gives you heartburn! Why don't we just all live on leaves and be done with it? Oh, I know why, because of the pesticides.

If I worried about everything I ate or every dust particle in the air, I wouldn't need to attract anything in my life because I wouldn't have the time to enjoy it. I understand warnings and cautions are in the best interest of the population.

However, I worry that focusing our worry and anxiety on every possible microbe in our environment or gram of fat in our food only makes us that much more susceptible to their potential ill effects. You've heard of hypochondriacs, right? These folks are convinced that they are sick, when in fact there's nothing medically wrong with them. The more you try to convince them they're all right, the more positive they are that they are dying.

I'm not likening anyone who's concerned about their cholesterol to a hypochondriac. I'm just saying that we see what we choose to see and focus our thoughts in that direction. So, instead of kicking yourself for eating that burger, and saying, "I'm killing myself!" say instead, "From now on, I will eat more healthful foods and improve my health by doing so."

The key is to have an understanding of certain conditions, but don't torment your conscience or you will make yourself sick and tired. Pay attention if you are told by reliable sources something is not healthy or is a risk to the body and the environment. But take that information and look at ways to neutralize or negate the potential harm. That's taking action in a positive way.

Take Action ... of Some Sort

Taking action is a marvelous thing to do when you're concerned with peace and environmental issues. But it needs to be something you take joy in, or else you are going against that feel-good energetic thing. If you participate in a group or organization that has a positive view about how to make changes to prevent climate change, for instance, and you are forcing yourself to go, that means you are not attracting better health to the planet. You're attracting the status quo or even worsening the situation.

You may not even realize it, but if you are doing something you feel you are forced to do, you are sending out negative vibes to all the others and to the universe that you don't want to be doing this. The universe will send you back a real whammy in the form of a worse situation. And perhaps just as bad, because others are picking up on your vibe, you may be influencing others to keep their distance from the planet's crisis, too. Find another activity that makes you happy, or give money to an organization that works to heal the Earth. (Hey, we're not all cut out to be in the trenches!)

Healing Rituals for Mother Earth

Many people believe in an appeal to the subconscious mind through rituals, a regularly repeated action or a series of actions intended to bring about a desired outcome. Many rituals focus on some sort of healing process and can focus on a person, place, or thing.

Many rituals are spiritual or religious. There are also daily things we do that can be considered rituals, like recycling.

What the Native Americans Know

Some Native American tribes perform rituals (like dance, fire ceremonies, or prayer) to bring forth rain, bountiful crops, and a multitude of other necessities that come from Earth. These rites were designed to bring up the consciousness and belief of those involved in them.

It is a collective effort to ask for what the community wants, and it is also a collective effort to believe it is going to come forth. Their emotions really get going—and, as you know, emotions are what fuel passion, and passion boosts your energy and request. This may sound like a contradiction to what I wrote about group appeals earlier in this chapter, when I said that it's difficult for groups to come together to ask for things because everyone has a different vision of how they see things or expect things, even though the main idea and goal is the same.

Here's the difference: in the past, the Native Americans lived very simply, and they didn't have as much information overload as we have available today. If they wanted rain, that's all they knew: rain. In a modern-day group when we think of rain, we might think, "We need rain … but not acid rain, and not too much rain because the houses in California might experience a mudslide."

The Native Americans knew that they needed rain for their crops or they would starve. Simple. Did their collective requests work? No one knows that for sure, but their approach was certainly more streamlined than anything we could achieve in this day and age.

"Comfort Food" for the Planet

You can conduct your own ritual to heal the planet if you want to. When I say the word *ritual*, that does not mean some shocking cult group who plucks chickens for feathers to use in their ceremonies. Brushing your teeth is a daily ritual for those of us who value our pearly whites. Coffee is a ritual for those of us who like that caffeine buzz. Life is filled with rituals.

Here are a few rituals you might want to try to help the planet help itself:

- Send the planet love by visualizing it encompassed by a healing light. Some may see it as blue or green; others might see it as white.

- Ask your higher power or source energy for the protection and the positive evolution of the planet and those people and situations that are not positive. Feel an upward shift and be happy when praying, not concerned or somber. Use words like, "May the planet be evolving in a positive cycle."

- Draw or find a picture of the planet and write the word *peace* on it. Every day just take a quick look and give it a thumbs-up or a big smile, and know it's already starting to happen.

As I always recommend, you can make up your own rituals. You are the creator of your own life, so in creating your own rituals, you share your genuine emotion and energy. It's okay to have fun with it! Fun is a positive feeling, after all, and that can lead you to repeating your ritual(s) over and over, creating a greater likelihood for success.

PART 5

Review Your Work

Some folks catch on to the law of attraction quickly and rarely experience disappointment or a sense of failure. For the rest of us, it takes time to perfect the methods of attracting and allowing. In these chapters, you'll troubleshoot common problems and also read about the best ways to help others by using the law of attraction.

CHAPTER 18

Helping Yourself and Others

Up to this point, I've talked about the law of attraction as it relates to you and your mind-set. Hopefully, you've learned that this is a powerful force that can bring very good or very bad things into your life, depending on what kind of energy you're sending out.

The law of attraction isn't always used for personal gain, however. Many people focus their energies on helping others. In this chapter, I'll talk about how to go about doing this without accidentally making matters worse.

Do Groups Attract More Quickly?

If one person can exude enough vibrations to get what he or she wants, what could a group do by working together for the purpose of achieving a goal? My goodness, think of the possibilities!

Well, actually, don't. Groups can be magnificent. A gathering of people enables different mind-sets and opinions to meld, which can result in astounding creativity. (Let's hear it for groups! Woo hoo!) This kind of sharing might work in brainstorming for a business venture. It may work well for rescue missions. It may work well for planning an event. But as far as using a group to bolster your intent, it just doesn't work very well.

Emotions Fly, Attraction Weakens

There is absolutely nothing like teamwork, people working together toward the same goal. In theory, you'd think that when people get together, the vibrations would be very strong. After all, the desire, excitement, and anticipation of so many should be able to give the vibration a huge boost.

Although this sounds like a great idea, especially when it comes to the law of attraction, in practice it rarely works. There are those who will feel as passionately about something as you do. There are those who will agree with you about some project or situation. There are even people who could finish your sentences because they look at life the same way you do. These folks have a true understanding of where you come from, what you have gone through, and perhaps even where you are going.

So, how can I say that likeminded friends can't boost intent by working together? Because no matter how much camaraderie exists within a group, no one can feel exactly what you're feeling. Have you ever been with someone who is very much like you, and yet has certain opinions and feelings about issues that you completely disagree with?

Everyone has his or her own unique guidance system or inner self. And their inner selves tell them something different from what your own inner voice tells you. That's the benefit of being human! We think for ourselves (or at least we should), and we each feel what we feel. There's no right or wrong ... it just makes us different from one another. And the universe responds to each of our unique vibrations in its own way.

When a group works together in a way that is more physical than emotional—say, planning a charity event—the vibrations are more general and unified and tend to work well. It's when a group tries to ask for abstract things, like world peace, that the varied vibes of the group are all over the map; hence, success is unlikely.

It comes down to this. When working in a group, people can get passionate, especially when they're focusing on an emotional issue like world peace or religious freedom. There is nothing wrong with being passionate, but all that emotion can send out conflicting vibrations and the results may end up being scattered, to say the least. The universe takes all those vibes, mixes them together, and sends back a response that may seem to be wildly off the mark. But how would you respond to all sorts of different energies coming at you like a Mack truck (the equivalent of a group's energetic vibe)? You'd do the best you could ... and so does the universe.

New Yorkers Team Up

A small group of men and women in New York did a little experiment trying to attract a new doorman for their condo. It wasn't that they hated their current doorman; he just wasn't the most pleasant person. The group also didn't want him to be out of a job or have anything bad happen to him. (They didn't want him to get hit by a truck so that, by default, he also wouldn't work in their building anymore, for example.) The goal was to envision him in a better position so that he would leave his current post behind.

The group sat together and visualized him in a better job setting and making more money. Everyone then asked this of his or her own personal source energy (God, higher power, etc.). Each member of the group used the same words and spoke at once.

This seems to make sense. It's an organized, calm grouping with a specific, rather generous vision. The problem was what each person felt about the doorman was different. When they said the words, they each had a different feeling about the desire:

- Candice wanted him out of that condominium because she thought he was rude.

- Bernard thought he was a pretty nice guy, but his dog didn't like him.

- Kevin actually liked the doorman, but he just wanted to go along with the crowd because it sounded like fun and he had nothing else to do that night.

- Marsha thought he was a flirt, but none of the other women in the group could see that side of him because she was the best-looking in the crowd.

- Sandra couldn't stand him because he reminded her of her ex-husband, Melvin. Although when she really thought about it, Melvin wasn't so bad. Maybe they could have worked it out.

Eek! As you can see, these emotions are far from unified, even though they're shooting toward a common target.

When they visualized him in his new job, things got even wilder. One saw him at a grand hotel in New York; someone else saw him in a condominium in California, and others just saw him in a doorway someplace—not anywhere in particular.

You can see where there would be some conflict in the vibrations the universe received. Even if the whole group had visualized the doorman in the same geographical location (Boston or Los Angeles, for example), each would have seen him wearing different clothes, experiencing different weather, standing in different-looking lobbies … and the list goes on.

So, what happened to the doorman? He's still there. He got a raise and the lobby got redecorated. In a way, they did get what they asked for. The one problem with this is that he's still downstairs in their building.

Understand, it's alright to talk with others about the law of attraction. You can discuss books and other tools that help you learn this universal law. But at the end of the day when it's time to get into asking mode, you need to stay independent. Focus your energy on your own intent and you'll have a better chance of success.

One Prize, Many Vibes

Attracting a first-place prize in a competition is the same as attracting good health, wealth, or a golf cart, for that matter. You have to desire it with all your heart and soul, you have to feel it and know this is what will make you happy, and you have to allow it to come into your life.

People who compete in contests usually want to win; otherwise, they wouldn't bother in the first place. Sure, there are some folks who enjoy the fun of the competition and don't care if they win or lose, but right now, we're going to focus on people who want that blue ribbon.

This is the story of the Florida Chili Cook-Off.

There was a cooking contest for the best chili this side of Alligator Alley in Florida. The competition was tough. There was Diver Dan with his Key West chili, which boasted a little bit of coconut. Then you had Pelican Pete with his Hurricane Chili with extra beans, which was always a windfall. And let's not forget Doris Taylor's chili, whose hotness was mostly attributed to cayenne.

These three really wanted to win this contest; it was more than fun—it was a real accomplishment, something they could use as a selling point in their various trades and businesses. Each could feel it in their inner beings that this was what they really wanted. Whether they were consciously using the law of attraction or not, they each sent out a vibrational signal for success that was bound to come back to them. Still, only one could win.

The concoctions were completed and in walked the judges. "Oh no," thought confident Diver Dan, "not him again! That guy's a joke. He doesn't like me because I put beer in my chili … the darn teetotaler. And like a ton of bricks, boom! Dan started thinking negative thoughts and severed his connection to that first-place title.

Next, Pelican Pete looked at all the judges and thought, "I think they will like my personality, so I may have a better chance than the others. Plus, I am all over social media these days. I think it's my bandanna that gets them. I hope something does, because the competition looks tougher than I thought." His personality was not what he was focusing on before the contest, so he switched his thoughts—and vibration—at last minute.

Doris Taylor saw that one judge looked like a sailor (his TopSiders and deep tan were dead giveaways) and that was it. She never liked sailors because she thought they were all cheap, like her ex-husband. She felt they liked sailing because the wind is free. (Now mind you, this is not my opinion. I love boaters.)

None of them won the contest. They let strong, negative last-minute vibrations come into the picture. They were more focused on who the judges were instead of the fact that their chili recipes were the best. (And for those who are wondering, the winner was Kyle Parker with his spicy cuisine!)

How 'Bout Just Two People?

Two can be as unfruitful as a group. Granted, there's less energy flying in different directions, but the results are usually about the same as a group experience: not completely satisfying, to say the least. Even if the person you're working with has been your best friend since kindergarten, your life experiences are not the same. The people you have met and the things you have done are not the same. Your past lives and lessons (if you believe in reincarnation) are not the same. So, your emotions and your vibrations cannot be the same.

Best Friends, Worst Vibes

The way you feel about the other person comes into play here, too. Even if someone is your best pal or favorite relative, there's always something about him or her you wish you could change—or some residual hard feelings about something he or she has no control over. For example, your friend may have just purchased a beautiful vacation home in Italy, while you're struggling to make the rent on your one-bedroom shoebox every month. You might say, "Wow, I'm really happy for you! How exciting!" And even though you don't wish for bad things to happen for her, you aren't exactly thrilled for her because you're jealous.

Your friend picks up on this and now she feels guilty for telling you she bought a second home. She feels sorry for you because you don't have more.

So, there sit the two of you, one envious and one feeling pity. And now you're going to try to attract a common request? It's not going to end well. Your vibrations have to be in perfect alignment, and even if you are close, it's still no cigar. Getting together with someone else to attract things in your life can be a riot; just don't expect much. I am not trying to be a pessimist, but it is universal law that you attract better on your own. Stick with get-togethers that make you happy, and you will attract more happiness for both of you. That's the best thing two people can do.

Coincide with Your Personal Energy Source

You can't run from everyone who doesn't agree with you. What you can do is avoid certain discussions with those people or find a way to agree to disagree. Look at Kellyanne Conway and her husband, George, who is an outspoken and public critic of Kellyanne's boss. No matter what your politics are or which of the Conways you're inclined to agree with, you have to admit that this would be a sticking point in a marriage. And yet somehow, they work it out and remain together!

Don't be so fragile that you run every time someone doesn't agree totally with what you have to say. If your thoughts are strong and you are crystal clear about what you want, you *will* succeed.

Help in Silence

As the law of attraction begins to work in your life, you may be so happy you have discovered this key to happiness that you want to tell the world. That's great if others want the knowledge—spread it around all you want. But if people are not interested, they may simply not be ready for the information, so stop yourself from sharing. Don't despair and feel as though you've somehow failed. There are other ways to help people, and they don't even have to know it.

Removing the focus of a person's dilemma and doing what you can behind the scenes using the law of attraction can be the best help you can give. Keep it simple when someone is in a stressful situation. Just a quick text or simple card that says, "I know things will turn around for you," can work.

Don't start with negatives like, "I am so sorry for the pain and suffering you must be experiencing."

You are starting your communication with negatives and that does not move anyone forward.

Is Your Inner Source Agreeing You Should Help?

You may be wondering how you can know whether you should lend a helping hand or stay out of another person's trouble. You can't help every person you run into, or go running to a complete stranger's house when a friend of a friend tells you about this person's sad plight. You certainly don't want to offer pity (because that only adds to the negative vibe of the situation), but what else can you do in these situations?

There is no magic to this. It's what I have been saying all through this book. You have to check to see how you really feel about it. The asking doesn't work if you don't feel it. So, if there is someone you think you might like to help but you still aren't sure, you can take time to assess what your actions should be.

First, simply think of the person and ask yourself how you feel. Do you feel sad for him or do you feel happy because you may think there is something you can do? Now you may feel blue at first, but then you might feel great joy when you actually think of the assistance you can give. However, if you feel that he is already in a situation that is hopeless and you aren't feeling confident that you can help, you probably can't.

Don't scold yourself for the way you feel. You can't fake it. The best you can do is be honest about your emotional inner self and what it's saying. Your source may be telling you there is someone who can offer more assistance and if you get involved, you would make matters worse.

On the other hand, if you sense that you can do something to help but aren't sure exactly what that is, then bring in the troops—that's right, use the law of attraction. Ask for clarity on what you can do to help. When you allow or receive your answers, take action with a positive attitude and with love.

Don't let them know that you have gone through much effort, if at all. If the person you've helped is going on and on about how wonderful you are to have assisted him, he may still be focusing on the problem, which should by now be in the past. Give him a gentle reminder to leave those hard times behind and concentrate on a positive future.

Include Others in Your Visions

There is a lot you can do to help others with the law of attraction, although these methods may not be traditional. I've just talked about taking action to help if you believe that you can, and if it feels right. But there is another way to help, and it may be the most powerful.

A forceful way to help someone on any level is to use the visualization techniques I talked about in Chapter 6. In your mind, just picture the person you are concerned about in a better state of being. If she is sick, see her healthy. If he needs money, see him debt free. If she requires something important in her life, see her with the things she needs.

Every morning take a few seconds and see the person the way you want him to be. You don't have to make it a drawn-out process; just stop while you're having coffee, for example, and think that the person is already healed, secure, or whatever is trying to be achieved. In your thoughts, you should not envision the person in his present situation. Instead, see that person as you want him to be—that's the believing part of the process!

Even if you meet someone for only a few moments and you wish you could help her right there and then, simply visualize the person in a better situation. You don't have to know her name or her history. Your higher power knows who you are thinking about.

If you were to stop and send good thoughts to everyone you see on the street, it would be overwhelming. So, visualize well-being for those who you really feel you are led to.

If you visit a friend in the hospital, don't look at the surroundings and fall into the "It's really too bad" mind-set. Rather, think about the joy he will have when he is discharged. And go one step further—see him discharged and cured. See him in the car going home and back to his normal life. Talk to him about what he is going to do when he gets out. Don't discuss all the other sick people and how so-and-so in the bed or room next door is even worse off. Talk about those Bucs, that latest book Diane Ahlquist wrote (ahem), or how you are going to take him to dinner when he's released.

Seeing people in an absolutely positive status in their lives is an exceptional way of assisting them. Not everything is judged in dollars and cents. Even when we have little in the way of material goods to give, we can do so much for others with our mere thoughts.

Seek No Appreciation

As I mentioned in Chapter 7, there's nothing wrong with helping people out, as long as your assistance is backed by compassion. But even when you're able to go way beyond anyone's expectations, don't make a show of it or look for accolades. By centering your thoughts on how you helped those who have nothing, you are focusing on what they don't have. By telling others and expecting applause and recognition, you are, in essence, asking others to focus on the situation you helped the person out of—and thus creating more of the same.

CHAPTER 19

Nothing Is Perfect

Nothing is perfect, but the law of attraction can be, if you understand it. But it's the understanding that can take a while. So, if it doesn't seem perfect, don't fret. It's not the law that's imperfect; it's your understanding of how it works in your life and in the universe.

You may be a little nervous about questioning the specifics of the law of attraction—after all, if you question it, that means you aren't believing it, right? Well, there are some common misconceptions about this process and I've personally never believed that ignorance is bliss. In this chapter, let's take a look at what some people consider to be the shortcomings of the law of attraction, and whether those things are truly deficiencies at all.

Negative Vibes Will Still Come a Knockin'

The law of attraction does work. I know it from my own experience and from the experiences of people who are close to me. Plus, the law of attraction has existed since the beginning of time, and humans have been harnessing it, using it, and sharing their methods with others for thousands of years.

Yet, the law of attraction doesn't equate with a perfect life. When folks first start to understand and use this powerful force, they often become frustrated because, even though positive things are starting to happen, there are still negative things going on in their lives. Is there really no way to get everything you want all at once? Is that the "secret" of the law of attraction, that you can only have one positive thing at a time? No! As you'll read in this section, learning to use the law can result in some mighty high expectations and disappointment when things aren't going as planned. Working your way around those emotions helps you get back on track faster.

Making Up for Lost Time

We can lose time thinking about why we still have negativity in our lives on one hand, while we are starting to attract what we want on the other. Sometimes I think people suddenly start to worry about what they don't have again because they have a fear of success. I am not a psychologist, but to those who are not used to getting what they want, when it suddenly starts to happen, it may be so unbelievable that they unintentionally sabotage what they have started. Maybe they feel unworthy, or maybe they're scared of the power of the universe. Whatever the reason, they put out a negative vibration that comes back to them, despite the fact that they're also concentrating on positive thoughts.

When success (or the beginning of what could be success), comes a knockin', open the darn door and allow it in!

Don't think about the things that haven't come into your life thus far, and don't think about how success is going to change everything. Focus on one thing at a time, or you'll never go anywhere or get anything you want. (Anything we ask for and receive could conceivably change our lives for better or for worse.)

You'll never be able to get back the time you've spent worrying about possible negative outcomes or not focusing on the things you want in your life. But you can save time in the future by not continuing to make these mistakes. Don't lament the fact that you didn't begin using this process sooner; be happy that you've found it *now!* And remember, as long as you still have breath in you, it's never too late to start using the law of attraction to fulfill your hopes and dreams.

The "Cancel" Method

Sometimes, as for everyone, my mind wanders all over the place. For no reason, I might start thinking about sad things that happened in the past or terrifying things that could possibly happen in the future. I try to stop myself and analyze what I'm imagining. Why am I having those thoughts when nothing special in life brought them on? Or perhaps something did bring them on, like an old song, a newspaper article, or a television show. It really bothered me to find I was spending time thinking about a situation, only to realize that the thought was completely negative. So, I came up with what I call the Cancel method.

Every time I start to have a thought or a daydream about something negative, I say to myself, sometimes out loud, "cancel".

It's like a thought starts to float up from my brain that is pessimistic, and by saying cancel, I grab it and stop it from going out to the universe. In other words, you are taking back your thought before it goes too far.

I have shared this method with readers before in other books and while lecturing. I am amazed at how many people have taken the time to experiment with it. From what I hear, it works for most. If that word doesn't work for you, try one of the following.

- Stop!
- Halt!
- Delete!

Just try not to use an entire phrase, like, "Wow, I wish I could stop thinking such sad thoughts. They really bring me down and make me wish I was happier." You're not accomplishing anything there except for making yourself feel worse. One-word cancellation thoughts are the best since they are fast and to the point. Sometimes people like to repeat the word two or three times in a row: "stop, stop, stop" or "cancel, cancel, cancel." This may depend on how strong and negative the thought is. Do whatever works for you.

Try it and see what you think.

Don't think you have to monitor every thought, or you will be "canceling" all day long. Use this method when your thoughts trouble you. For example, say you're at work and your coworker is someone you really don't care for. You have the thought, "I would love to see her suddenly grow a mustache," and suddenly you think, "That wasn't very nice. I have to cancel that out." Fear not; she will not grow a mustache anytime soon. Thoughts have to be focused regularly to come into fruition. No one is perfect—even the folks who've been using the law of attraction for decades make the occasional slip-up. Be human (not superhuman) and do the best you can with your best efforts.

When Intentions Backfire

Whenever you are *not* creating with deliberate intention, you might end up with a great big surprise and not necessarily a pleasant one! When you put out the directive that you want something, you should be very confident that this is what you really want. This is no time to be nonchalant. When you're creating what you want, take time to evaluate it before you ask for it. Visualize what you want, and really, truly see it through from beginning to end (or as far as is reasonable). What you want one day may change the next. Or once it starts to come your way, you may see where it's going and decide this isn't for you at all.

Don't make hasty decisions. You're the one who wanted that job at the new bookstore because it's a place to meet people, the coffee is free, and you love books. Sounds like a good plan. Suddenly, there you are, working in the back most of the time. You don't meet anyone, you drink so much coffee with creamer that you gain 10 pounds, and you are too tired to read at the end of the day. Oops! Maybe you should have included in your intention that you wanted to work up front and the workload would be reasonable. (And the creamer? What can I tell you? Perhaps they have a low-cal version that really appeals to you. If not, visualize the creamer having no effect on your weight.)

Sometimes the devil is in the details, so I cannot emphasize it enough: think before you ask.

Does the Law of Attraction Work for Evil?

Throughout this book, I've told you that the universe doesn't know the difference between what you *do* want and what you *don't* want. It simply gives you what you give your attention to the most. Therefore, to answer the question, can the law of attraction be used for evil? The unfortunate answer is yes. The good news is that positive thoughts seem to vibrate stronger than negative thoughts. A lot of focusing would have to be given to intentionally create negativity, although it can be done.

Don't assume someone can create bad things in your life. He cannot if you don't allow negative thoughts in. For example, if you're auditioning for a commercial and you keep thinking that some other actor (a guy who just hates you with a passion) is going to get the job instead of you, change your thoughts. If he's thinking negative thoughts about you, and you allow those thoughts in, then by worrying about it, you are helping him get the job instead of you. Rather, think things like, "So? I don't care who this guy likes or doesn't like; it doesn't affect my life."

Now as far as conjuring up evil spirits or forces … that's not the law of attraction. This may be a misperception among folks who are afraid of energies that aren't labeled by a religious tradition, but I can assure you, the law of attraction is not easily used by those who want to bring harm to others.

Bear in mind, the law of attraction is always working whether you believe it or not. It is your gut feeling and your internal message source that tells you if something is right or wrong. What overrides your intention is when the source sees that you are not in harmony or in vibrational alignment with what you want. You need to fine-tune yourself with your desire by allowing it to come into your life without doubt or hesitation.

Does This Come with a Guarantee?

I can guarantee you that the law of attraction works—as long as are willing to put the time and effort into deciding what you want, asking for it with no reservations, believing that it will come to you, and receiving it into your life when you see your request beginning to come to fruition. Let's take the commercial audition example from earlier in this chapter. Let's say that you have asked the universe to help you land this job, and as you made your request, you thought to yourself, "If this doesn't work, then I'll know this law of attraction is a bunch of bunk." With that last thought, you have attached a negative vibration to your request, and guess where that's going to get you? Nowhere—and fast!

Posing a request as an "or else" statement—I'd better get what I want, or else I'll tell everyone I know that this universal theory is nonsense!—pretty much negates everything you're asking for. You can't *test* the universe; you're the one who will fail each and every time. Think of this in terms of challenging other forces of nature. Would you challenge a grizzly bear to a wrestling match? Would you try to swim the Atlantic to prove a point? Would you stand outside in a Category 5 hurricane to show that nothing is more powerful than you are? Just as I can guarantee you that you will lose each of these scenarios, I can guarantee that surrendering your supposed "power" to the universe will bring you triumphant results.

The reason we want guarantees is because we want to be covered in case of a breakdown. Well, the law doesn't break down … we do. If you want a sign-sealed-delivered type of guarantee, buy a new refrigerator. Otherwise, learn to trust and believe in the power of the universe. Once you can do that, you will never be disappointed.

Real People, Real Results

I love real-life stories, as you may have noticed by now. Therefore, I am including some success stories of people who were kind enough to share their experiences. I could write an entire book on the subject alone. However, I chose stories with a variety of subject matter.

The best I can wish for you is that someday you, too, have a success story you want to share with others. It is stories like these that give us hope and inspiration. So, I thank all who've allowed me to include their tales.

Diane's Personal Story

I wrote a different version of this book a long time ago and have practiced these teachings for quite a while. But as a human, sometimes I, too, lose my way. I took myself out of alignment with source energy. Time seemed to push me one way or the other, and I wasn't putting attention into meditation, contemplation, and being focused on the law of attraction like I had been.

Recently, I was under contract to write a new book for another publisher having nothing to do with the Law of Attraction and had normal deadlines and was writing away. But, prior to that, I'd had some health issues, was trying to sell our house, and nothing was going right. My office is part of my laundry room, so while doing laundry and writing, I needed more space and decided to take some papers and put them on the top shelf of my bookcase. And, there it was, my old book *The Law of Attraction*, which was not on my mind at all.

What in the world have I been thinking? Most things in my life were good as I had programmed the law of attraction in my mind by now, but I was not thinking about it daily. I put the book back and thought, I will renew my practices shortly after my obligations are fulfilled. I didn't have time to think about it at that point.

I was pondering thoughts like, "Better rush in case my computer gets a virus, or my electric goes out," as it does this time of year in Florida due to weather. Well, of course, the universe heard me and said, "Okay you want the computer to get a virus and your electric to go out? Done!" I was nearly 50 percent finished with my manuscript and my computer got a virus. I don't print things out or save things on flash drives, etc. I just leave them on my desktop and know they will be okay because my computer loves me. Yet, my computer got a virus, and in order to save time, I called a computer guy to come to my house. He said no way could my work be retrieved. Other than a few things I did print out, I had to start over rewriting from scratch.

Now, trying to tell an editor this is like saying the dog ate your homework. No writer would be so careless or irresponsible, but I attracted it with my negative thinking. I take full responsibility! About a week later, after trying to get back on track with the book, I was nearly done and needed a few more hours, and our electricity went out. I called the power company and we were the only ones who had a power outage. (And yes, we pay our bills.) There was no way I could tell the editor that one. Four hours later, the electricity came back on, and I continued to write.

All I could think was, "I need to move my office because what happens if this washing machine springs a leak." Well, you guessed it—water all over! As I continued to eat glazed doughnuts and drink coffee while writing a book about well-being, it occurred to me that I have to change my thoughts. (Is it a bad sign when your carpenter says, looking down at the doughnuts, he can widen the office door if need be?)

What happened to the law of attraction I used to live my life by?

I switched my thoughts and decided to read my own book again. Every time I started reading, something stopped me, and I didn't really have the time. I kept thinking that I would feel so much better once I reread my book, and I started getting myself back to normal. I could feel myself getting happier at the thought that I would be back on track. But I still didn't have the time to really go through that law of attraction book.

I asked the universe to lend a hand. I believed I would find the time and then I thought something would happen to open up more time for me. In other words, I started to lift my vibration and my mood with positive thoughts and happy emotions. A couple of days later, out of the blue, my agent contacted me to let me know that a publishing company (this one) contacted her and wanted me to update this book, *The Law of Attraction!* It would force me to remember, read, and reboot. And, so I did. The universe answered me.

Marie's Recipe for Receiving

I have a friend named Marie who was trying to practice the law of attraction, and she had it down! She thought seriously and logically about what she wanted. Then she checked her inner self to see if she felt right about what she wanted, and she got the go-ahead. Marie wanted to recover from her smoking addiction. When she thought about being cigarette-free, it made her smile. She thought she would never have to spend money on smokes ever again, so even her finances would benefit. Plus, no more ashtrays to clean; no more stinky house. Even her yellow cat might get back to her original white color.

There were so many pluses; she was happy as a pig in mud.

She knew what she wanted and did her universal asking when she was in a good mood. She believed. She already ordered new carpet because the old one had smoke imbedded in it. She set up an appointment in one month for her small cat, Virginia Slim, to have a complete beauty treatment and cleaning at the Diva Pet Spa. (Virginia was the replacement cat for the one who ran away; he was named Winston.) Marie was smokin', but without tobacco.

She had no struggle at all, not the first day or any day after that. She was so busy planning her new smoke-free life that she couldn't even think about cigarettes. The days rolled by, and on the third week of being cigarette-free, she told a friend about her success using the law of attraction. Her friend said, "Don't want to burst your bubble, but you are ready for a big let-down. You can't stop smoking with no problems. You have to go through all kinds of stuff. You are addicted to nicotine, and you can't get rid of an addiction without going through withdrawals and suffering. It will not be easy. It took me 2 years to do it, and you are a worse smoker than I was."

Now Marie could have easily grabbed on to this doubt and negativity and let it drag her down, but she wasn't having any part of that! Marie didn't listen to her friend, and guess what? She didn't suddenly regress—she got rid of the friend. Now she and her white cat, Virginia Slim, are living a healthy, smoke-free life in a clean home. She got into alignment with who she is, and she liked herself.

Henri Has It All Now

Henri was a French interior designer living in New York. He was creative, artistic, and forever looking for a partner. No one ever really ended up staying with him.

He did very well financially (he kept $3,000 in an Eiffel Tower cookie jar!), but he never thought it was enough. He didn't look at his personality or his spirituality—everything was all about money to him. So, he worked to get more money, but even when the Eiffel Tower was stuffed like a crêpe, he still wasn't happy because he was all alone.

Being an intelligent and open-minded individual, and being a user of the law of attraction and very committed to the philosophy, he did something with a bit of a twist. Instead of asking the universe for a mate, he asked to learn the reason why no one ever came into his life who wanted to stick around and make a life with him. He visualized, and he chanted, "I see London, I see France, why do I not have romance?"

After 3 weeks, he started to understand what the problem was. Someone told his boss that the guy with the beret had great design talent but was lacking in people skills, and of course, his boss shared this news with Henri. His boss shared this with him at about the same time Henri was hired—as luck (or the law) would have it—to create a Zen space for a couple in Brooklyn. This gave him time to reflect on the importance of listening to that inner voice and hearing what feels right as far as intention goes.

Henri realized that his dates and mates had not been interested in his money, and that he wasn't the easiest person to be around. He had to change his outlook and reevaluate the important things in life if he wanted to share his life with someone. His new desire was to become a better and more understanding person.

Henri now still resides in the Big Apple but he is no longer alone. He no longer judges his prosperity in dollars and cents, but in understanding. Oh, and the cookie jar is now stuffed with labels from bottles of Chardonnay.

Common Misconceptions

Sometimes people think that because they read a book or watch a video they are on their way to putting the law of attraction into action. They may understand the theory and even agree with it. But then they forget about it and put it into the positive-thinking category. I have often heard people say, "Oh, I get the law of attraction. It's basically about positive thinking, and I have always been a positive thinker. There are lots of books out about positive thinking; I remember when I read a book back in the day …," and the story goes on. These people are remembering what they once read and even once practiced, and think the law of attraction is a good reminder of what they already know, but they are not following the detailed plan. They are seeing the glass half full instead of half empty and that's just not enough.

If you take the idea into your own hands and tweak it, that's one thing. But if you generalize and think you know it all, that can mean failure.

Here are some misconceptions about the law of attraction, followed by my comments about each one:

- By wishing and praying every day and really being positive, you can get what you want. That's all you need—positive thought.

- Comment: That's a good start, but remember, you have to feel it, and allow the process into your life.

- If you get what you want, you have to share what you know about the law of attraction with other people because if you don't, it's selfish.

- Comment: Of course, you should share with others if you think it can help them. But if they are not serious or open minded, it's more selfish to annoy them and shove your beliefs down their throats.

- It takes an exact time frame to get what you want.

- Comment: How can we say something will take 20 days or 30 days? It will take however long it takes, but again, it's all in the believing.

- If I really ask, believe, and allow, I never have to work again. I just have to stay home and think.

- Comment: This sounds like a challenge to me, and a sarcastic statement. Very few people believe this—and remember how I talked about how we have to take action? You won't want to sit; source energy will give you desire to walk the road and experience the journey.

The most important part of misconceptions, I think, is to separate them from the facts. It's alright to question how the law of attraction works—that's just part of learning about it. As long as you keep a positive perspective on your questions, you aren't engaging in doubt! And if you do find yourself heading toward doubt, use that Cancel method again when you find yourself buying into these half-truths and outright errors.

CHAPTER 20

Doubling Down on Requests

Okay, you may be reading this last chapter just to finish the book, as you have already started attracting what you want. Or you may be reading this chapter thinking, "Well, I tried everything that Diane Ahlquist told me to do and nothing happened!" Now you're hoping to find the solution to where you went wrong. If this is the case, you might understandably be a little disappointed. The law of attraction is a promise akin to Christmas morning, after all—the hope of getting everything you've ever wanted in a timely manner!—and to have that promise fade and dwindle (or crash and burn) is disheartening.

But here's the thing: the law of attraction doesn't fade, dwindle, or crash and burn. When we find it isn't working for a specific request, there's usually a specific reason that you can attribute it to. What are those reasons? Well, I talked about them throughout the book, presented more as what *not* to do than as specific reasons for failure. In this chapter, we'll take a look at some of these common mishaps and how to prevent yourself from inadvertently putting them into practice.

Let's Look Back

At the beginning of this book, we discussed that you need to decide what you want, not what you don't want. Then the next step is to believe that it can happen. And finally, you have to allow yourself to receive what you have asked for. So, the first thing to ask yourself is whether you've followed the steps as you must.

Deciding with Confidence

You may think you were confident when you decided what you wanted. But what one person calls confidence, another might call haste, and yet another might call wishy-washy.

Did you sit down and take time to really focus on just one or, at most, a few things at a time? Or, as is the case with many people who become so excited about the law of attraction, did you ask for 50 things at once? Let's go with the benefit of the doubt and assume that you did in fact decide with confidence to ask for only one or two things at a time and you haven't seen any results. How did you make the decision of what to ask for? Answer the following questions:

- Was it something you have been wanting for years?
- Was it something you just thought about recently?
- Were you too general, such as "I want to be rich"?
- Were you too specific, such as "I want to marry Billy"?
- After you made your decision, did you change your mind and then ask for something different or in another way?
- Did you write your request down to be absolutely clear, or did you just think it in your head?
- Did you discuss your decision about what you wanted with others and ask for their opinions?

Hmmm ... so what's the problem with some of these issues? Well, as I said in Chapter 19, if you've wanted something for years, it's possible that you've been sending out conflicting vibes without even knowing it. It's just going to take some time for the universe to sort through the confusion surrounding your request. Keep on sending positive thoughts, though, and you'll get what you want.

And when you're looking for love or companionship, you're wise not to name names. Don't choose a specific person; rather, focus on the characteristics of your ideal partner. Is your desired mate funny, serious, smart, kind, musical, and so on?

I have said it before, and will say it again, you cannot make someone else love you. The other person has his or her own energy and goals to stick with, and if those goals don't mesh with yours, you'll start to doubt yourself—hence, confusion, doubt, and negativity will surround your request (and it won't come to fruition). You are not a vibrational match.

Believing with Emotion

Let's say you made your request and you really did (and do) believe that the law of attraction could work for you. But did you feel it with that butterflies-in-your-stomach feeling or with the anticipation and excitement of knowing a great event was going to take place?

This is where many people go astray. They think their request is right because they want it to be right, but they don't have that physical passion that tells them this is something that's really worthwhile. It's like going to dinner with someone who only looks at you as a platonic friend when you want more. You are excited to be with that person, and you are hoping it will turn into something more. But deep down in your heart, you are still doubtful that anything will happen because this person has never shown romantic interest before. And so you're excited about the possibility, but you fear the final outcome won't be what you want.

Reception without Doubt

So, you say that you really, truly wanted what you asked for, and you tapped into your passion and emotion. Did you allow yourself to receive your request, or are you subconsciously afraid of how your life will change if your hopes come to fruition?

Earlier in this book, I said that you wouldn't keep flagging down your waiter and ordering a meal over and over again until the food comes. You order once and then accept the fact that your food will be coming soon. You don't sit there watching the kitchen door, worrying that you're never going to eat again, that you're going to starve, that the waiter didn't hear you, and that you need to tell him what you want one more time.

So, ask, feel it, allow it, and believe that it will happen. Just accept it! And don't sit around worrying about what you should do while you wait, because in doing that, you're focusing on the lack of whatever it is you're waiting for. Be happy, go about your life, and know that your request will come to you.

The Law of Attraction Didn't Work for Me!

Let's say you have gone through the process as you should, and you feel you did everything correctly. Let's go one step further. Perhaps other than this book, you bought all the other law of attraction books with basically the same information, presented differently. And mercy, you have seen all the YouTube videos presented so eloquently and informatively. You may have even have taken classes and seminars about the law of attraction, and still, zippo, nada, zilch. Is it you, or are these authors and speakers full of malarkey?

Saying "It Doesn't Work" Makes It So

If the law of attraction hasn't worked for you yet, you are probably saying or thinking many things, none of them particularly positive. But recall that you get what you ask for if you believe it. And if you are at the point where you really don't believe and you feel this is a bunch of hooey, you are feeding fuel to the negative fire. Try to avoid thinking and feeling any of the following:

- ♦ "This just doesn't work."
- ♦ "I think it can work, but I must be doing something wrong. I'm just going to forget it if nothing happens soon."
- ♦ "If it's too good to be true, it probably is."

◆ "I'm so glad I didn't tell any friends or family I was trying this; I would have looked like a fool."

◆ "Maybe I am just expecting too much too soon."

I understand how your frustration is made worse by the idea that you may be on the brink of something powerful. If you aren't seeing results, you may be angry (that others have had luck with the law of attraction); you may feel foolish for investing time and belief in something that apparently isn't going to work out for you; and yet you wonder, if it has worked for people throughout the ages, why can't it work for you?

The best advice I can give you is to stop questioning the process, because by doing so, you're effectively telling the universe that you don't trust it. The universe, remember, doesn't punish doubt—it simply gives you the same vibe you send out.

Were You Trying Too Hard?

If you have been trying too hard to make your request manifest itself into reality, you will feel it in the form of law-of-attraction burnout.

Never heard of this affliction? You will feel like you are trying to convince yourself that any time now, your wants and desires are going to happen. You may also feel that you are really trying to be positive—you smile, wish, hope, and plan—but, again, without feeling the true emotion behind those gestures. Also consider the fact that you may have been overthinking and trying too hard.

It may be time to lie low for a while. It's alright to take an "attraction vacation" if you feel like you're getting burned out or overly obsessive waiting for your requests. Both of these emotions are quite negative, obviously, and breaking that cycle might help your cause immensely.

Take a different approach and stop thinking about your request, even in a positive way. Focus on something else altogether—and I don't mean something else that you want. Read a book or take a trip. Take some mental time off, and don't ask for any other requests for at least a week.

How many times have things like these happened to you?

- You get done writing a long email or text and before you hit send … they call you.

- You adopt a child and then miraculously become pregnant.

- You finally buy new clothes because you will never lose weight and then you drop a dress size.

- You sell your ex-fiancée's engagement ring for half price, and she comes back to you. (You should have let her keep it in the first place, Cheapo!)

Once you give up on something, or once you just stop thinking about it (which is better in this case—never give up!), it may come to you quickly. The reason is because you stop thinking about the lack of the thing you want and, *ta da!* You have switched your focus, and that might be just what you need.

See the Signs

Sometimes people will think that they are not getting anywhere with the universe and start looking for signs of encouragement. If you stop and pay attention, you're likely to see positive symbols of success as you come closer to your goal.

Let's use a legal issue. Suppose you have a lawsuit pending and you have been waiting for a decision in the case. The lawyers don't return your calls, and things seem to drag on and on. Suddenly, you are sitting next to someone on the train who tells you about a lawsuit he just won. Then when you go home and flick on the television, there is a movie on with a plotline about a lawsuit.

The next thing you know, you get an ad on your text for the "Legal Beagle." (I am assuming there is no law firm out there with that name, and if there is, you're wonderful.)

It's like the universe's email to you that says, "I'm a comin' with your judgment about this case, and it's good!"

Don't Start Over, Start from Here

The thought of starting over after you have put so much energy and effort into attracting what you want may seem like too much work, especially if you feel you've been let down by the universe. And I don't blame you for not wanting to do it.

But you don't really have to start over. Remember, you already have started paving the way. You just need to get a grip on what kind of detour you're on (and why). Your choices are to remain off the path of your intention or to find your way back onto it. Which is it going to be?

Read Your Daily Journal

If you have been keeping a daily journal about your intents and attempts to bring what you desire to fruition, go back and read it. Remember, people have been keeping journals since the beginning of time. Writing is a wonderful way to organize your thoughts and to literally see your progress. Just remember to focus on the positive events of the day!

Can you find any clues that tell you where you may have taken one step forward and two steps back? For example, did you quiet your mind and concentrate on asking for a new job, but instead of using the word *want*, you phrased it as a *need*? Remember, we attract the vibration we put out, and "need" is a negative vibration. It indicates that there's a lack in your life … and so, lack is what you get back.

Don't linger too long on the negative events or circumstances, but if you could change something about the way you've approached the universe, what would it be?

Read Your Achievements

Now let's look at your achievements in that same journal.

How do those make you feel? From the day you began focusing your intent, what have you done each day to ensure success? Have you taken time to visualize a positive outcome? Have you used daily affirmations to move your desire along? Are you doing everything in your power to have a positive outlook? Are you ready and willing to accept your desire into your life?

If you've accomplished these major tasks, then relax and be happy. There's nothing more you can do to keep on keepin' on and know, without a doubt, that the universe is listening and working on a response. Be happy!

Not a Journal Keeper? It's Not Too Late to Begin!

If you are not a person who likes to write down the details of daily happenings, you can take a spiral notebook or a legal pad and just jot down a few things that you think are bringing you closer to your goal. Use your iPad and create a new note titled "daily journal" or whatever you like to call it.

Use a calendar with tiny squares and write a few words about something that reminds you of something good that happened that day: "Dog got better" or "No headaches today."

The point of keeping a journal is to remind yourself that good things are happening—maybe they seem small and insignificant today, but as time goes on, having a written record enables you to look back and say, "Oh my gosh! There's a definite pattern going on here! This is really happening!" Just like that, your belief is bolstered, and your vibrations become stronger and more positive. Guess what that means? Your desire moves that much closer to reality.

Even if you don't have a lot of newsworthy events to report in your journal, at least find a way to end each day on a happy note. Think about one good thing that happened, even if it's that you got the last piece of apple pie at the restaurant, or the fact that you still have a roof over your head.

Writing things down—even briefly jotting down a note here and there—helps you remember those positive little things. That's the mind-set you want to have when you are trying to attract something, even if it's sporadic at first. People who've been down in the dumps for a long time can especially benefit from this type of work. It can take a long time to turn your outlook around—why not use every tool at your disposal (and especially one that's so easy)?

Rework Your Plan

In Chapter 19, I talked about whether there is a power out there that can override your request. My answer was that if you are in alignment with your request, the answer is no. But do bear in mind, you have to be in total alignment with your desire. (In other words, you know it's the best thing for you, you back it with emotion, and you believe that it can and will happen.) So, if your request hasn't happened, maybe you did nothing wrong at all, at least as far as the universe is concerned. If you don't feel it, the universe won't send it. It's like a system of checks and balances.

If you seem to be attracting most of what you want with a few exceptions, those exceptions may not be in harmony with your vibe, and it's best to understand it might not be for you at all.

If you're not feeling it, it's like your inner guidance system is saying, "What part of this don't you understand? This just isn't for you!" This doesn't happen because the universe doesn't want you to have your desire, but because your vibration isn't in sync with what you think you desire. So, how do you get into that vibration? You really can't force yourself. If all of the pieces aren't fitting together because of something that's going on with your life or even because of your fundamental beliefs, then you may just have to set the request aside for now and come back to it at a later date.

You could also say to the universe, "If it's not in alignment with my intent, send me another thought or intent that is." You can do this with people, jobs, spiritual endeavors, and even health issues. You may want to land an appointment with the best surgeon in the country and you just can't get in. Override that request by asking for a doctor who is best for you, and you will align faster with that energy or person.

Why Timing Is Important

Sometimes you don't necessarily need an override; you just need to regroup and let life go on for a while and try again. It's like your motor might be overheated, and if you leave it alone for a while, it will work when you try to start it up again.

This is why it is so important from the get-go to see if your desire and request really feel right for you. They need to be in alignment. Some people go against their inner voice and end up terribly disappointed when they don't get what they asked for. They are in resistance of the flow. You can't put a square peg into a round hole. If it's not right, then you should thank your higher power that you *didn't* get it!

Also remember that if you want to achieve a goal by a specific date, you can ask that you get what you want in a certain time frame. If you're not sure what is reasonable, then ask for clarity on what is a reasonable amount of time for this project or request. You cannot take too big a jump. You don't go from weighing 190 pounds to your goal weight of 120 in one day. The universe has the ability, but remember you have been programmed for years and years to know that even if you don't eat for 24 hours you don't lose 70 pounds overnight.

Making a Few Small Adjustments

Have you been using the suggestion I mention in Chapter 10 about breaking your day up into divisions (morning, afternoon, and evening)? If you aren't remembering, on a daily basis, to start your day with thoughts of your desires, then start tomorrow! This helps to reinforce your positive energy, belief, and intent by making your request(s) more realistic in your mind. If you don't believe your requests are reasonable things that can happen, then they won't.

For example, if you want to pass a test at the end of the month, then each morning you might think as you get out of bed, "I am going to read one page of my notes. I want to remember what I read." The next thing you know, it's test day, and because every day you've been laying a brick on that road to success with your intention, you pass with flying colors. (Inch by inch, attraction's a cinch!)

Some people tend to get thoughts that are too overwhelming for their subconscious minds, as well. Let's say that you and your sister have not spoken in 10 years— and who remembers why anymore? What feels better? Asking the source that you and your estranged sister suddenly become friends again overnight, or requesting that when you call her, she is open to talking things out? Don't defeat your goal by asking for what your logical mind doesn't think can happen. After the small things start to come into fruition, you'll know how to phrase your requests so that they come at a comfortable pace for you.

Mark Twain, American author, humorist, and lecturer, put it fittingly when he said:

> The secret of getting ahead is getting started. The secret of getting started is breaking your complex, overwhelming tasks into small, manageable tasks, and then starting on the first one.

Let Your Feelings Be the Decision-Maker

There are only a few people out there who can project their vibrations so strongly that they can sit back and do nothing of a physical nature to make their desires come to fruition. Does that make them better than us? No, it just makes them free of living in a society that teaches us that hard physical work is the only way to be happy. Those of us (and that would be most of us) who have been programmed to believe we have to do a little something to get something back are just as capable of tapping into the power of the universe and using it to our benefit.

No matter which way you go about using the law of attraction or how much physical or mental work you have to put into it, remember to call on your inner source to guide you toward what's right for you. Although source energy is all-powerful, you are the cocreator of your life and your reality, so what you say goes. The universe depends on you knowing and feeling what's best before you ask for it, so evaluate, visualize, ask, believe, and allow … and enjoy the ride.

We are on this planet to learn lessons and gain knowledge, or we would not be here. Therefore, don't expect to be perfect when using the law of attraction. We are all learning and that's part of the joy!

Glossary

affirmations   Repeated, positive thoughts used to increase the likelihood of success or happiness. Also referred to as *autosuggestions*.

compassion   A sincere desire to understand the plight of others and to help them without pitying them.

energy   Refers to the vibration that each person emits. Vibration is either positive or negative; thus, energy is either positive or negative.

higher power   An expression used to describe a power greater than yourself; this could be a power such as God or your personal inner being.

karma   The belief that what we do in this lifetime dictates what will happen to us in our next lifetime. It is a Hindu belief, based on the idea that our souls travel on and into another life form at the time of physical death. *See also* reincarnation.

law of attraction   The belief that one receives the same type of energy that one puts out to the universe; "like attracts like." *See also* universal law.

law of cause and effect   Any action creates a reaction that's equal in strength and energy; e.g., a positive action will garner an equally positive reaction.

law of gratitude   The belief that you can't truly learn from any situation—positive or negative—unless and until you can appreciate what you've learned from it. *See also* universal law.

law of love   The acknowledgement that we are all part of one universe, and we must learn to accept one another as is. *See also* universal law.

lemniscate   A figure-eight symbol turned on its side, which often represents infinity; this symbol is sometimes used as a focal point when one is clearing one's mind.

meditation   A way of calming the mind and body so that you can focus on a specific thought.

new age   A set of beliefs that center around the planet, the universe, and their collective energy.

numerology   An ancient study and application of the meaning of numbers and how they pertain to and influence your life.

personal power or **energy source**   What some people call *Spirit* or their inner essence; it gives you the strength to attract positive things to your life. *See also* Spirit.

programming   Refers to the thoughts we're trained to believe about ourselves and the world around us, even though they may not be true.

reincarnation   The idea that after someone dies, his or her soul lives on and eventually returns to this life in another human form to learn and grow. *See also* karma.

ritual   A regularly repeated action or series of actions intended to bring about a desired outcome.

source or **source energy**   Refers to the nonphysical root of all things in the universe; the power or presence that resides over all things.

Spirit   Sometimes referred to as one's essence or inner being; it is our source of strength and the origin of our true nature.

universal law   Truths that have always existed and do not change with time. *See also* law of love, law of gratitude, *and* law of attraction.

universe   The source of all personal energy and power; the all-encompassing energy that affects each one of us.

vibration   The type of energy each of us emits to the universe; you receive the same type of vibration back from the universe.

vibrational match   Can be positive or negative. "Like attracts like." "That which is like into itself is drawn." What you think about, you bring forth.

visualization   A method of engaging the mind to imagine a particular outcome.

Resources

In the introduction to this book, I said that this isn't the first book written about the law of attraction; I also said that this topic is open to more than one interpretation. For those of you who are yearning to read more about the law of attraction, I've compiled a list of books and websites here for easy reference. Happy learning!

Books

Besant, Annie. *Thought Power*. Daly City: Book Tree, 2004.

Bristol, Claude M. *The Magic of Believing* (Original Classic Edition). New York: G&D Media, 2014.

Byrne, Rhonda. *The Secret*. Hillsboro, OR: Beyond Words Publishing, 2006.

Byrne, Rhonda. *The Magic*. New York, NY: Atria Books, 2012.

Denning, Melita, and Osborne Phillips. *Practical Guide to Creative Visualization*. St. Paul: Llewellyn Publishing, 2001.

Hicks, Esther, and Jerry Hicks. *Ask and It Is Given: Learning to Manifest Your Desires*. Carlsbad: Hay House Publishing, 2004.

Hicks, Esther, and Jerry Hicks. *The Law of Attraction: The Basics of the Teachings of Abraham*. Carlsbad: Hay House Publishing, 2006.

Hooper, David. *Guide for Living: Law of Attraction Workbook—A 6-Step Plan to Attract Money, Love, and Happiness*. N.P.: Kathode Ray Enterprises, LLC, 2007.

Just, Shari L., and Carolyn Flynn. *The Complete Idiot's Guide to Creative Visualization*. Indianapolis: Alpha Books, 2005.

Kingma, Daphne Rose. *Finding True Love*. Berkeley: Conari Press, 2001.

Losier, Michael J. *Law of Attraction: The Science of Attracting More of What You Want and Less of What You Don't*. New York: Grand Central Life & Style, 2010.

Madison, Mark. *The Complete Self-Help Guide on How to Manifest Anything in Life and Attract Wealth, Health, and Happiness.* Independently published, 2018.

Ray, James Arthur. *The Science of Success: How to Attract Prosperity and Create Harmonic Wealth Through Proven Principles.* La Jolla: SunArk Press, 1999.

Stapely, Louise. *Law of Attraction: 30 Practical Exercises.* CreateSpace Independent Publishing Platform, 2015.

Digital Resources

dianeahlquist.com   Author's website with information on the law of attraction, events, and her other books.

Divine Imagination with Joseph Alai   This is a YouTube channel featuring new videos related to the law of attraction every other day. You can also browse through an extensive archive of videos.

drwaynedyer.com   Self-help and self-development guru. His site includes podcasts, videos, and writings on using the law of attraction to invite everything you want into your life.

louisehay.com   Founder of Hayhouse Publishing, Louise Hay's work was based on spirituality and raising one's vibration to the highest level.

Michael-losier.mykajabi.com   Michael Losier's site about the law of attraction, including online courses, one-on-one coaching, links to Facebook discussions, and in-person events.

Mindbodyspirit.com   A YouTube channel featuring videos about attracting anything and everything you've ever wanted into your life.

thesecret.tv   This website is related to the book *The Secret* by Rhonda Byrne regarding the law of attraction.

Worksheet to Aid in Goal-Seeking

When you're trying to get a grasp on an abstract concept, sometimes it helps to write things down. This is especially helpful when trying to sort out the things you really, truly want. Throughout the book, I've mentioned putting pen to paper. To make it that much easier, you may want to complete this worksheet.

For clarity, let's start off with how you got to where you are now. You don't want to dwell on it, but being aware of it can help you not to make the same mistakes in the future. If something does not apply to you, simply leave it blank.

Once you have filled in the declaration section (or all the number 1s), go back and fill in the number 2s. Then go back and fill in the number 3s, and finally, the number 4s. Don't fill them in all at once. Take time to think and regroup upon rereading.

The General Issue That Weighs Heavily on Your Mind

Think about a concern that is weighing most heavily on your mind right now.

1. **Right now, the thing that dominates my mind (only pick one) or I am concerned about the most is ...**

_____

_____

_____

This statement makes me feel ...

_____

_____

_____

I feel this way because ...

_____

_____

_____

This is what I am going to do to make it better or to keep it the same:

_____

_____

_____

2. I have been thinking strongly about this for _____
(amount of time).

This statement makes me feel ...

_____

_____

_____

I feel this way because ...

_____

_____

_____

This is what I am going to do to make it better or to keep it the same:

_____

_____

_____

Now let's look at other areas of your life. Think before you write, and concentrate on your answers.

Health

Let's start with the most important topic, which, to me, is your health.

1. When I think about my health I am pleased because ...

_____

_____

_____

This statement makes me feel ...

_____

_____

_____

I feel this way because ...

_____

_____

_____

This is what I am going to do to make it better or to keep it the same:

_____

_____

_____

2. **When I think about my health, I am not pleased because ...**

_____

_____

_____

This statement makes me feel ...

_____

_____

_____

I feel this way because ...

_____

_____

_____

This is what I am going to do to change it:

_____

_____

_____

Finances

Be honest about your finances. If you are doing well financially, don't search for things that may be a problem because you feel guilty about your success. Write about your present situation.

1. When I think about my financial situation, I feel good because …

_____

_____

_____

This statement makes me feel …

_____

_____

_____

I feel this way because …

_____

_____

_____

This is what I am going to do to make it better or to keep it the same:

_____

_____

_____

2. When I think about my financial situation, I feel bad because ...

_____

_____

_____

This statement makes me feel ...

_____

_____

_____

I feel this way because ...

_____

_____

_____

This is what I am going to do to change it:

_____

_____

_____

Intimate Relationships

You may or may not have an intimate relationship at this time. Some of you may have several going at once. No one is judging you, so be as honest as you can.

1. When I think about my relationship(s), I feel happy because …

_____

_____

_____

This statement makes me feel …

_____

_____

_____

I feel this way because …

_____

_____

_____

This is what I am going to do to make it better or to keep it the same:

_____

_____

_____

2. When I think about my relationship(s), I feel unhappy because …

_____

_____

_____

This statement makes me feel ...

_____

_____

_____

I feel this way because ...

_____

_____

_____

This is what I am going to do to change it:

_____

_____

_____

3. **When I think about not having a relationship at all in my life, I feel joy because ...**

_____

_____

_____

This statement makes me feel ...

_____

_____

_____

I feel this way because ...

_____

_____

_____

This is what I am going to do to make it better or to keep it the same:

_____

_____

_____

4. **When I think about not having a relationship at all in my life, I feel frustrated or sad because ...**

_____

_____

_____

This statement makes me feel ...

_____

_____

_____

I feel this way because ...

_____

_____

_____

This is what I am going to do to change it:

_____

_____

_____

5. Because I have intimate relationships with more than one person, I feel totally comfortable because …

_____

_____

_____

This statement makes me feel …

_____

_____

_____

I feel this way because …

_____

_____

_____

This is what I am going to do to make it better or to keep it the same:

_____

_____

_____

6. Because I have intimate relationships with more than one person, I feel uncomfortable because ...

_____

_____

_____

This statement makes me feel ...

_____

_____

_____

I feel this way because ...

_____

_____

_____

This is what I am going to do to change it:

_____

_____

_____

Platonic Relationships and Friendships

Write about any other type of relationships you have—friends, relatives, working relationships, and so forth—any relationships that are not of a romantic nature (even your pets). I have included extra sections, as you may have many relationships. Use additional paper if you run out of space.

1. **When I think about my relationship with** _____,
   I focus on ...

   _____

   _____

   _____

   This statement makes me feel ...

   _____

   _____

   _____

   I feel this way because ...

   _____

   _____

   _____

   This is what I am going to do to make it better or to keep it the same:

   _____

   _____

   _____

2. **When I think about my relationship with** _____,
   I focus on ...

   _____

   _____

   _____

   This statement makes me feel ...

   _____

   _____

   _____

   I feel this way because ...

   _____

   _____

   _____

   This is what I am going to do to make it better or to keep it the same:

   _____

   _____

   _____

3. **When I think about my relationship with** _____,
   I focus on ...

   _____

   _____

   _____

This statement makes me feel ...

_____

_____

_____

I feel this way because ...

_____

_____

_____

This is what I am going to do to make it better or to keep it the same:

_____

_____

_____

4. **When I think about my relationship with _____,**
   I focus on ...

_____

_____

_____

This statement makes me feel ...

_____

_____

_____

I feel this way because ...

_____

_____

_____

This is what I am going to do to make it better or to keep it the same:

_____

_____

_____

5. **When I think I have no friends or relationships at all, I know this is because ...**

_____

_____

_____

This statement makes me feel ...

_____

_____

_____

I feel this way because ...

_____

_____

_____

This is what I am going to do to change it:

_____

_____

_____

Career/Job

Sometimes we love our jobs or career, and sometimes we need to make changes. If you're in the latter category, then this section is for you!

1. The job that I am in now never causes me worry because ...

_____

_____

This statement makes me feel ...

_____

_____

I feel this way because ...

_____

_____

This is what I am going to do to make it better or to keep it the same:

_____

_____

_____

2. The job that I am in now makes me worry because ...

_____

_____

_____

This statement makes me feel ...

_____

_____

_____

I feel this way because ...

_____

_____

_____

This is what I am going to do to change it:

_____

_____

_____

3. I have more than one job because ...

_____

_____

_____

This statement makes me feel ...

_____

_____

_____

I feel this way because ...

_____

_____

_____

This is what I am going to do to change it:

_____

_____

_____

4. I think I should look for a second job because ...

_____

_____

_____

This statement makes me feel ...

_____

_____

_____

I feel this way because ...

_____

_____

_____

This is what I am going to do to change it:

_____

_____

_____

5. **I don't have a job at all because ...**

_____

_____

_____

This statement makes me feel ...

_____

_____

_____

I feel this way because ...

_____

_____

_____

This is what I am going to do to change it:

_____

_____

_____

6. I don't want to work at all because ...

_____

_____

_____

This statement makes me feel ...

_____

_____

_____

I feel this way because ...

_____

_____

_____

This is what I am going to do to change it:

_____

_____

_____

Home or Living Arrangements

1. The place I live now is acceptable because ...

_____

_____

_____

This statement makes me feel ...

_____

_____

_____

I feel this way because ...

_____

_____

_____

This is what I am going to do to make it better or keep it the same:

_____

_____

_____

2. The place I live now is not acceptable because ...

_____

_____

_____

This statement makes me feel ...

_____

_____

_____

I feel this way because ...

_____

_____

_____

This is what I am going to do to change it:

_____

_____

_____

3. In the future, I want to move because ...

_____

_____

_____

This statement makes me feel ...

_____

_____

_____

I feel this way because ...

_____

_____

_____

This is what I am going to do to make it happen:

_____

_____

_____

4. I am thinking about moving to ... _____.

This statement makes me feel ...

_____

_____

_____

I feel this way because ...

_____

_____

_____

This is what I am going to do to make it better or to make it happen:

_____

_____

_____

Following are two examples of how a section may look with the added text underlined.

Home or Living Arrangements

1. I am thinking about moving to <u>not sure</u>.

   This statement makes me feel <u>confused and lonely</u>.

   I feel this way because <u>I can't make a decision, and no one seems to be able to help me or give me answers that make sense</u>.

   This is what I am going to do to change it: <u>Because I am not sure what I want, I am going to use the law of attraction to attract the answer to me. When I know what I want, I can proceed from there.</u>

Intimate Relationships

1. When I think about not having a relationship at all in my life, I feel joy because <u>all my relationships have been a disaster, and I can't go through that again</u>.

   This statement makes me feel <u>relieved that I have made that decision. You don't have to have an intimate relationship to be happy. It's just not for me.</u>

   I feel this way because <u>my friends in relationships always have some type of problem with their partners. I'd rather be alone! It just sounds like too much trouble, and it makes me feel nervous thinking about catering to someone else. I love my own company and if other people don't agree, I can't worry about their opinions. This is what makes me happy!</u>

This is what I am going to do to make it better or to keep it the same: <u>I am avoiding relationships and focusing on my work and my animals. I get plenty of love from other people and things in my life. I will keep attracting love and companionship in my life from other means. I will continue to attract peace and comfort.</u>

Once you are done with the exercise, you should have a grasp on what you want, how you feel, what you like and dislike, and how you are going to start changing it, if that's what you choose to do.

Every week or so, look back at your statements. On a separate piece of paper, write what has changed and why. Just write it as though you are writing a story. You do not need to answer any questions.

It should read something like this:

> *I wanted the job downtown working for the computer manufacturer. I did not get it, and I was disappointed.*

> *Then I realized that when I was asking, it never felt right in the first place. I tried to push it and kept asking, but nothing happened. Then when I asked for the job at the stock-brokerage firm, it just felt better.*

> *I forgot I needed to listen to my gut when I was looking for my desires. In fact, the job at the brokerage firm made me feel all warm and fuzzy, as they say, whenever I even thought about it.*

> *I really felt that job was right. Therefore, the vibration went forth like a locomotive and I nailed the interview and am working there now, and I'm happy.*

INDEX

V

W–X–Y–Z